University of New England
Teaching Monograph
7

ABORIGINES
IN COLONIAL SOCIETY
1788-1850

Other titles in the Series

1. R. Harrold, *Economic Thinking in Education* (1982).

2. W.S. Simpkins, A.R. Thomas and E.B. Thomas (eds.), *Principal and Task: An Australian Perspective* (1982).

3. H.E. Doran and J.W.B. Guise, *Single Equation Methods in Econometrics: Applied Regression Analysis* (1984).

4. G.E. Battese, *Introductory Statistics for Economic Studies* (1986).

5. R.J.S. Macpherson, *Ways and Meanings of Research in Educational Administration* (1987).

6. W.S. Simpkins, A.R. Thomas and E.B. Thomas (eds.), *Principal and Change: The Australian Experience* (1987).

Alphonse the Tasmanian
(from a 19th century drawing by T. Napier)

Aborigines in Colonial Society: 1788-1850

From 'Noble Savage' to 'Rural Pest'

Second Edition

Edited with an introduction by

Jean Woolmington

Lecturer in History

THE UNIVERSITY OF NEW ENGLAND
AUSTRALIA
1988

© Jean Woolmington and University of New England, 1988.

This work is copyright. Apart from any fair dealings for the purpose of private study, research, criticism, or review, as permitted under the Copyright Act, no part may be reproduced by any process without written permission. Inquiries should be made to the publishers.

Printed by the University of New England,
    Armidale, NSW, 2351.

Distributed by the University of New England Publishing Unit
    University of New England
    Armidale, NSW, 2351.

First published 1973
Reprinted 1974
By Cassell Australia Limited
As ISBN 304 29960 X

University of New England Teaching Monograph Series
ISSN 0726 156 X

Cataloguing-in-Publication entry

Aborigines in colonial society, 1788-1850.

    2nd ed.
    Bibliography.
    Includes index.
    ISBN 0 85834 747 4.

    [1]. Aborigines, Australian, Government relations — History.
    [2]. Aborigines, Australian — Treatment — History. I. Woolmington, Jean, 1927-
    (Series: University of New England teaching monograph; 7).

323.1'19915

Contents

Preface to Second Edition	iii
Acknowledgments	v
Abbreviations	vii
Introduction	ix
1 Official Policy	1
2 The First Contacts	13
3 Breakdown of Official Policy	34
4 The Aborigines' White Problem	57
5 The Public Conscience	74
6 The Work of the Missionaries	85
7 The Protectorate	106
8 Aborigines and British Justice	127
9 The End of an Era	146
Selected Secondary Sources	155
Index	157

Preface to Second Edition

In the fifteen years since this collection first appeared attitudes to the Australian Aborigines have changed quite markedly, and with them the language we use. While our forebears spoke of bringing the benefits of civilization to the Aborigines, we recognise that they have developed a perfectly legitimate civilization of their own over the thousands of years before Europeans arrived.

I am glad to have had the chance to rewrite some of the linking comments and to correct a couple of errors which had slipped into the original edition. My thanks go to Lynette Riley-Mundine, the Aboriginal Research Fellow at the University of New England, for her help in identifying language which may now have caused offence. The documents have not been altered, of course, and many of them appear even more stark than they did when the compilation was originally made.

Jean Woolmington
University of New England, 1988.

Acknowledgments

I am indebted to the following libraries and institutions for permission to reproduce manuscripts and other materials. The Public Record Office, London (the Bonwick Transcripts); The Church Missionary Society, London (C.M.S. microfilmed archives of the Australian and New Zealand Missions 1804-84); the National Library of Australia, Canberra (Diary of Mrs Christiana Brooks, a photo-copy of which is held by the Library: the original is in the possession of Miss A.C. Moriarty of Goulburn, N.S.W.); and the Mitchell Library, Sydney (Aborigines, Papers; W.W. Burton, Papers Relating to Aborigines 1796-1819; James Günther, Correspondence 1826-78; Dr J. D. Lang, Papers; Archdeacon T. H. Scott, Papers; and William Watson's Diary).

I should also like to thank Bruce Mitchell and Stephen Foster for their valuable help and criticism during the preparation of the manuscript.

The detail from Augustus Earle's 'Natives of N. S. Wales. As seen in the Streets of Sydney' (front cover) is reproduced from *Views in New South Wales and Van Diemeen' Land,* Australian Scrap Book 1830, by courtesy of the Trustees of the Mitchell Library, Sydney. 'Alphonse, the Tasmanian' (frontispiece) is reproduced from a 19th century drawing by T. Napier, J.P..

Abbreviations

B.P.P.	British *Parliamentary Papers*
C.M.S.	Church Missionary Society
H.R.A.	*Historical Records of Australia*
H.R.N.S.W.	*Historical Records of New South Wales*
L.M.S.	London Missionary Society
M.L.	Mitchell Library
N.S.W.L.C.V.P.	*New South Wales Legislative Council Votes and Proceedings*
W.M.S.	Wesleyan Missionary Society.

Introduction

From earliest times governors of British colonies and settlements were instructed to treat indigenous peoples with friendliness and kindness; to protect and to defend them; and to punish any settlers who did injury to them. When Englishmen settled in eastern Australia the attitude of the home government towards the Aborigines followed this tradition, as may be seen in the instructions to Governor Phillip and his successors.[1] Most of the early governors tried to follow these instructions, but all failed.

By 1850 it was generally accepted that the Australian Aborigines were a dying race; moreover, that they *had* to die because they had shown themselves incapable of adapting to white man's civilization. Indeed, their decay had been predicted for some time.[2] In 1849 William Charles Wentworth declared in a debate in the New South Wales Legislative Council that the civilized people had come in and the savage must go back; in the same debate Robert Lowe said, 'Let these benighted tribes be taught how immeasurably inferior they were in every respect to civilized men'.[3] That the Aborigines were so regarded by responsible citizens sixty years after the foundation of settlement is indicative of the great gulf that had come to exist between the Colonial Office and the colonists, and between the local executive and the colonists.

This book describes, by means of government documents, missionary journals, private letters and diaries, and colonial newspapers, the development of this gulf. It aims to explain why the breakdown of Aboriginal tribal life and traditions occurred when colonial governors had been instructed to protect them. Emphasis is laid upon the attempts made by colonial officials, by individuals and by missionary societies to avert this disaster, or at least to ameliorate the sufferings of the Aborigines. Reasons put forward for their failure

[1] See Documents 3 and 4.
[2] See Chapter 4, section 2.
[3] *Sydney Morning Herald*, 29 June 1849.

are examined. The British humanitarian movement's attempts to influence Australian attitudes to the Aborigines is a necessary part of the story.

It was a story repeated in much the same way throughout Australia. Space does not permit a detailed study of every colony, and for this reason examination is confined to that area known up to 1850 as New South Wales (frequently referred to as New Holland); that is, an area which included the present Queensland, New South Wales and Victoria.

Referring to this episode of Australian history one author recently wrote:

> ... I think that the emptiness of conscience and compassion that made the melancholy business tolerable had something to do with our racial views later.[4]

The documents quoted in the following chapters illustrate that emptiness of conscience and compassion, and show that the earliest white Australians, in their attitudes and behaviour on racial matters, were not so very different from later Australians who formulated and implemented the 'White Australia' policy.

Jean Woolmington
University of New England, 1973

Note: The editor has retained original spelling and punctuation. Interpolations appear in square brackets.

---

[4] W. E. H. Stanner, 'Australia and Racialism', in F. S. Stevens (ed.), *Racism: The Australian Experience*, Vol. 1, Sydney, 1971, p. 11.

I
Official Policy

Traditional attitudes

During the 1830s in Britain, much concern was expressed by humanitarians for native peoples throughout the world, particularly those within the British Empire. Slavery had been ended in 1833 but still there was concern that native peoples were being maltreated. In 1835, a House of Commons Select Committee began to collect evidence from people with experience of the indigenous populations of British Settlements, and in 1837, almost half a century after the settlement of New South Wales began, they published their Report. They had indeed found the worst fears of the humanitarians to be true, and the Committee believed that, although excuses might have existed in the past, none could be made in 1837.

1   Great Britain has, in former times, countenanced evils of great magnitude—slavery and the slave trade; but for these she has made some atonement; for the latter, by abandoning the traffic; for the former, by the sacrifice of 20 millions of money. But for these offences there was this apology; they were evils of an ancient date, a kind of prescription might be pleaded for them, and great interests were entwined with them.

An evil remains very similar in character, and not altogether unfit to be compared with them in the amount of misery it produces. The oppression of the natives of barbarous countries is a practice which pleads no claim to indulgence; it is an evil of comparatively recent origin, imperceptible and unallowed in its growth; it never has had even the colour of sanction from the legislature of this country; no vested rights are associated with it, and we have not the poor excuse that it contributes to any interest of the state.[1]

The claim that maltreatment of natives had never had even the colour of sanction from the legislature of Britain would appear to be true. Earlier in the Report the Committee referred to an address by Charles II

---

[1] Report from Select Committee on Aborigines (British Settlements), 1837, *B.P.P.*, (425), Vol. VII, p. 75.

to the Council of Foreign Plantations, and quoted it (with interpolations) to illustrate that Great Britain had never been disposed to sanction unfair dealings.

2 'Forasmuch as most of our said Colonies do border upon the Indians, and peace is not to be expected without the due observance and preservation of justice to them, you are, in our name, to command all the governors, that they, at no time, give any just provocation to any of the said Indians that are at peace with us,' &c.

Then, with respect to the Indians who desire to put themselves under our protection, that they 'be received.'

'And that the governors do by all ways seek firmly to oblige them.

'And that they do employ some persons to learn the languages of them.

'And that they do not only carefully protect and defend them from adversaries, but that they more especially take care that none of our own subjects, nor any of their servants, do any way harm them.

'And that if any shall dare to offer any violence to them in their persons, goods or possessions, the said governors do severely punish the said injuries, agreeably to justice and right.

'And you are to consider how the Indians and slaves may be best instructed and invited to the Christian religion, it being both for the honour of the Crown and of the Protestant religion itself, that all persons within any of our territories, though never so remote, should be taught the knowledge of God, and be acquainted with the mysteries of salvation.'[2]

The instructions given to Governor Phillip by George III had many similarities to those of Charles II, although they did not mention Christianity.

3 You are to endeavour by every possible means to open an intercourse with the natives, and to conciliate their affections, enjoining all our subjects to live in amity and kindness with them. And if any of our subjects shall wantonly destroy them, or give them any unnecessary interruption in the exercise of their several occupations, it is our will and pleasure that you do cause such offenders to be brought to punishment according to the degree of the offence. You will endeavour to procure an account of the numbers inhabiting the neighbourhood of the intended settlement, and report your opinion to one of our Secretaries of State in what manner our intercourse with these people may be turned to the advantage of this colony.[3]

[2] *ibid.*, p. 4.
[3] *H.R.N.S.W.*, Vol. I, Part 2, p. 89.

All the subsequent governors of New South Wales up to and including Sir Thomas Brisbane,[4] were given exactly the same instructions. Only with the appointment of Governor Darling in 1825 did the official instructions concerning the Aborigines change, as did the Governor's instructions on many other matters, following the Bigge Reports. Conversion to Christianity once more became a policy as it had been when Britain's American Colonies were founded in the 17th century.

4 ... it is Our further Will and Pleasure that you do, to the utmost of your power, promote Religion and Education among the Native Inhabitants of Our said Colony, or of the Lands and Islands thereto adjoining; and that you do especially take care to protect them in their persons, and in the free enjoyment of their possessions; and that you do by all lawful means prevent and restrain all violence and injustice, which may in any manner be practised or attempted against them; and that you take such measures as may appear to you with the advice of Our said Archdeacon to be necessary for their conversion to the Christian Faith and for their advancement in Civilization.[5]

A significant point to be noticed is that Charles II referred to British colonies bordering upon the lands of the Indians. This concept does not appear to have been held in the Australian situation. Perhaps the observations of Captain Cook in 1770 explain this.

5 Neither are they very numerous, they live in small parties along by the Sea Coast, the banks of Lakes, Rivers creeks &c. They seem to have no fix'd habitation but move about from place to place like wild Beasts in search of food, and I believe depend wholy upon the success of the present day for their subsistence.... In short these people live wholy by fishing and hunting, but mostly by the former, for we never saw one Inch of Cultivated land in the whole Country.[6]

Cook, in fact, took possession of the whole of New South Wales in the King's name.

6 Notwithstand[ing] I had in the Name of His Majesty taken possession of several places upon this coast, I now once more hoisted English Coulers and in the Name of His Majesty King George the Third took possession of the whole Eastern Coast from the above Latitude [38° South] down to this place by the name of *New South*

---

[4] *H.R.A.*, I, x, p. 598.
[5] Darling's instructions, *ibid.*, xii, p. 125.
[6] Cook's Journal, 23 August 1770, in J. C. Beaglehole (ed.), *The Journals of Captain James Cook*, Cambridge, 1968, p. 396.

Wales, together with all the Bays, Harbours Rivers and Island situate upon the said coast. . . .[7]

> This claiming of the land, coupled with the belief that the Australian Aborigines did not use it, was to be the root of much future trouble in New South Wales. However, this Colony was not alone in treating the natives' rights to their lands with contempt, as the 1837 Report indicated.

7 It might be presumed that the native inhabitants of any land have an incontrovertible right to their own soil: a plain and sacred right, however, which seems not to have been understood. Europeans have entered their borders uninvited, and, when there, have not only acted as if they were undoubted lords of the soil, but have punished the natives as aggressors if they have evinced a disposition to live in their own country.[8]

> The official stand, then, was that the native peoples had to be protected, befriended, uninterrupted in their pursuits and that they had rights to the soil. The conversion to Christianity was a later concept on the Australian scene. The official attitude to New South Wales will now be examined in some detail.

New South Wales

> Captain Arthur Phillip, while waiting to sail for New South Wales, put forward various suggestions concerning the running of the settlement. Among them was his plan for dealing with the Aborigines.

8 I shall think it a great point gained if I can proceed in this business without having any dispute with the natives, a few of which I shall endeavour to pursuade to settle near us, and who I mean to furnish with everything that can tend to civilize them, and to give them a high opinion of the new guests, for which purpose it will be necessary to prevent the transports' crews from having any intercourse with the natives, if possible. The convicts must have none, for if they have, the arms of the natives will be very formidable in their hands, the women abused, and the natives disgusted.[9]

> The Colony could not have been supervised by a more humane Governor, yet difficulties with the natives began very early in his period of government (see Chapter 3).
> While the instructions were given to each governor upon his appointment, it was still necessary for the Colonial Office to draw special attention to them at times. In 1802 the Secretary of State for the Colonies wrote to Philip Gidley King, the Acting Governor:

---

[7] 22 August 1770, *ibid.*, pp. 387–388.
[8] Report from the Select Committee on Aborigines (British Settlements), *loc. cit.*, p. 5.
[9] Phillip's suggestions, 1787, *H.R.N.S.W.*, Vol. I, Part 2, p. 52.

9   Before I dismiss this subject, I cannot help lamenting that the wise and humane instructions of my predecessors, relative to the necessity of cultivating the good-will of the natives, do not appear to have been observed in earlier periods of the establishment of the colony with an attention corresponding to the importance of the object. The evils resulting from this neglect seem to be now sensibly experienced, and the difficulty of restoring confidence with the natives, alarmed and exasperated by the unjustifiable injuries they have too often experienced, will require all the attention which your active vigilance and humanity can bestow upon a subject so important in itself, and so essential to the prosperity of the settlement, and I should hope that you may be able to convince those under your Government that it will be only by observing uniformly a great degree of forbearance and plain, honest dealing with the natives, that they can hope to relieve themselves from their present dangerous embarrassment.

It should at the same time be clearly understood that on future occasions, any instance of injustice or wanton cruelty towards the natives will be punished with the utmost severity of the law.[10]

Within the Colony frequent proclamations were made by the various governors concerning relationships with the Aborigines.

Proclamation

10   By His Excellency Philip Gidley King Esq. etc. Whereas a Despatch by the Coromandel has been received from the Principal Secretary of State for the Colonies, containing His Majesty's Commands, That notwithstanding His permitting the Governor to Remit the Punishment of the five Persons tried by a Court of Criminal Judicature on the 18th of October, 1799, for wantonly killing Two of the Natives, yet 'It should, at the same time, be clearly understood that on future occasions any instance of Injustice or wanton Cruelty towards the Natives will be punished with the utmost severity of the Law'; And His Majesty having at the same time recommended that every means should (after the Receipt of those Despatches) be used to conciliate the Goodwill of the Natives, I do hereby strictly forbid any of His Majesty's Subjects, resident or stationary in this Colony, from using any act of injustice or wanton Cruelty towards the Natives, on pain of being dealt with in the same manner as if such act of Injustice or wanton Cruelty should be committed against the Persons and Estates of any of His Majesty's

[10] Lord Hobart to Acting Governor King, 30 January 1802, *H.R.A.*, I, iii pp. 366–7.

Subjects; But at the same time that His Majesty forbids any act of Injustice or wanton Cruelty to the Natives, yet the Settler is not to suffer his property to be invaded, or his existence endangered by them; in preserving which he is to use effectual, but at the same time the most humane, means of resisting such attacks. But always observing a great degree of forbearance and plain dealing with the Natives appears the only means they can adopt to avoid future Attacks, and to continue the present good Understanding that exists.[11]

> The treatment of Aborigines was not only a matter of Government orders and proclamations. They were also remembered in such day to day matters as Port Regulations. The following was issued in 1810 and the authors evidently saw no need to explain the obvious contradiction between their order that the natives were to be treated as Europeans 'in every respect', yet were to be forbidden to purchase or accept alcohol.

11 . . . The natives of this territory are to be treated in every respect as Europeans; and any injury or violence done or offered to the men or women natives will be punished according to law in the same manner and in equal degree as if done to any of His Majesty's subjects or foreigners residing here; and no spirits, wine, beer, or other intoxicating liquor is to be sold or given from on board any vessel to a native.[12]

> As we have seen, the instructions given to Governor Darling included taking measures to convert the Aborigines to Christianity with the aid and advice of Archdeacon Scott. The Archdeacon began his task by setting a survey in motion.

12 I have the honor to acquaint Your Excellency, for the information of His Majesty's Government, that, in obedience to the King's Command, signified under the Royal Instructions, bearing date the 17th July, 1825, an extract from which Your Excellency was pleased to transmit to me for my guidance, requiring that I should take measures for the civilization of the Black Natives of this Colony and their conversion to Christianity. I have selected a Person well qualified for that task; and I have sent him into a part of the Country, where he can most probably obtain information relative to the state of these people, both from Persons, who have been long resident there, and from the tribes themselves.

I have at the same time written a letter to several of these Gentlemen, who have not only taken a great interest in the subject, but have tried the experiment in various ways, requesting their opinions;

---

[11] *ibid.*, pp. 592–3.
[12] Port Regulations and Orders for ships in Port Jackson, 1 October 1810, *H.R.N.S.W.*, VII, p. 418.

and, as soon as I am enabled to form a report from these documents, I shall lose no time in laying it before Your Excellency.

I, however, consider it necessary to state, in this early stage, that a very considerable expense must be incurred to do anything effectually, inasmuch as many Establishments must be formed in various parts of the Colony according to the number of the Tribes; and His Majesty's Government should be apprized of this, as well as the fact that, at a large expense, I have been hitherto quite unable to afford sufficient spiritual or Scholastic attention to those born of European Parents and others, even by requiring from the Clergy duties more severe than any Clergyman goes through in England, inasmuch that the Services of two have been suspended through indisposition in consequence of the late intense heats; and perhaps it would be desirable for Your Excellency to take the pleasure of His Majesty's Government, how far they are disposed to authorise so large an expenditure, which must necessarily reduce the funds set apart for the instruction of the Colonists.[13]

Scott's cautious approach to spending money on converting the Aborigines while many whites were living in spiritual poverty was fully appreciated in Westminster. Nevertheless the Colonial Office believed that the ground-work should still be done.

13 There can be no question as to the importance of a measure which would contribute to the happiness and comfort of so large a body of people by withdrawing them from the wandering life which in their present uncivilized state, they must necessarily lead; but, whilst due attention is paid to this desirable object, others of comparatively greater importance must not be neglected; and as a difficulty is already felt from the want of adequate funds in providing the necessary religious Instruction for the benefits of the Colonists generally, I need not point out to you the expediency of suspending for the present of any extensive exertions, leading to expense, which it might otherwise be expedient to use in favour of the Aborigines of New South Wales. The Archdeacon's proceedings should, therefore, be confined to obtaining correct information as to the numbers and conditions of those people, in order that the Government may be prepared with the means of adopting more effectual measures, in furtherance of the object in contemplation, whenever circumstances shall admit of the formation of the Establishment which the Archdeacon is of the opinion will be necessary for that purpose.[14]

[13] Scott to Darling, 9 December 1826, *H.R.A.*, I, xii, pp. 796–7.
[14] Goderich to Darling, 6 July 1827, *ibid.*, xiii, pp. 433–4.

Once mission stations were established, the official policy was one of assistance and co-operation as far as possible. In answer to a letter from D. Coates, Secretary to the Church Missionary Society, concerning the grant made to that Society to run a mission to Aborigines, Under-Secretary Twiss wrote:

14 The Society will probably consider it a sufficient security to be informed that it is the present intention of Government to continue the grant so long as they shall have reason to think that the mission is conducted with propriety, and with some reasonable prospect of ultimate success. That this success is not to be expected within any short period they are perfectly aware.

. . .

You further desire to be informed whether the extension of the mission be in the intention of Sir George Murray, should its progress be satisfactory, and facilities and encouragements grow out of its operations.

Upon a question so general and indefinite it is not in the power of the Secretary of State to furnish an answer. It may perhaps, however, be sufficient for the purpose of the Church Missionary Society to be assured that the conversion of the Aborigines of New Holland to christianity, and the introduction of civilization amongst them, is regarded by His Majesty's Government as an object of so much importance that there is no probability that any undertaking which held out a fair prospect of success would be permitted to languish for the want of additional pecuniary aid.[15]

Concern for the welfare of the Aborigines of Australia, and indeed for indigenous peoples in all British settlements, was expressed in an address passed unanimously by the House of Commons in July 1834.

15 That His Majesty's faithful Commons in Parliament assembled, are deeply impressed with the duty of acting upon the principles of justice and humanity in the intercourse and relations of this country with the native inhabitants of its colonial settlements, of affording them protection in the enjoyment of their civil rights, and of imparting to them that degree of civilization, and that religion, with which Providence has blessed this nation, and humbly prays that His Majesty will take such measures, and give such directions to the governors and officers of His Majesty's colonies, settlements and plantations, as shall secure to the natives the due observance of justice and the protection of their rights,

---

[15] Horace Twiss to D. Coates, 18 February 1830, Papers relative to the Aboriginal Tribes in British Possessions, *B.P.P.*, 1834 (617), Vol. XLIV, p. 150.

promote the spread of civilization amongst them, and lead them to the peaceful and voluntary reception of the Christian religion.[16]

> This address was sent in a circular to the Governors of all British colonies, including Governor Bourke of New South Wales.[17]
>
> Yet, as we saw at the beginning of this chapter, in spite of government instructions and financial support; in spite of the unanimous resolution of the House of Commons and the efforts of colonial governors, it became necessary in 1835 to hold a Select Committee of enquiry into the treatment of native peoples in British colonies.
>
> The responsibility Britain held towards native peoples was emphasized in their Report.

16 We are apt to class them under the sweeping term of savages, and perhaps, in so doing, to consider ourselves exempted from the obligations due to them as our fellow men. This assumption does not, however, it is obvious, alter our responsibility; and the question appears momentous, when we consider that the policy of Great Britain in this particular, as it has already affected the interests, and, we fear we may add, sacrificed the lives, of many thousands, may yet, in all probability, influence the character and the destiny of millions of the human race.[18]

> Looking more specifically at the Australian Aborigines, the Select Committee asserted that the coming of the white man had affected them most cruelly.

17 The inhabitants of New Holland, in their original condition, have been described by travellers as the most degraded of the human race; but it is to be feared that intercourse with Europeans has cast over their original debasement a yet deeper shade of wretchedness.

These people, unoffending as they were towards us, have, as might have been expected, suffered in an aggravated degree from the planting amongst them of our penal settlements. In the formation of these settlements it does not appear that the territorial rights of the natives were considered, and very little care has since been taken to protect them from the violence or the contamination of the dregs of our countrymen.

The effects have consequently been dreadful beyond example, both in the diminution of their numbers and in their demoralization.[19]

> One point made strongly in the Report was too late to have effect in much of eastern Australia.

[16] Report from the Select Committee on Aborigines (British Settlements) 1837, *loc. cit.*, pp. 4–5.
[17] W. W. Burton, *Papers relating to Aborigines*, MSS. No. A1161, M.L.
[18] Report from the Select Committee on Aborigines (British Settlements) 1837, *loc. cit.*, p. 3.
[19] *ibid.*, p. 10.

18   This, then, appears to be the moment for the nation to declare, that with all its desire to give encouragement to emigration, and to find a soil to which our surplus population may retreat, it will tolerate no scheme which implies violence or fraud in taking possession of such a territory; that it will no longer subject itself to the guilt of conniving at oppression, and that it will take upon itself the task of defending those who are too weak and too ignorant to defend themselves.[20]

> The problem of alcohol had already been felt in New South Wales by the time the Select Committee's Report appeared. Nevertheless, the attention of local governors was drawn to the need to make as much effort as possible to overcome the problem.

19   The prohibition of the sale of ardent spirits, or the delivery of them to the natives in barter, is an object of the deepest interest, which it is, therefore, impossible to pass over in silence; at the same time, it is vain to deny the extreme difficulty of rendering any such prohibitory rule effectual, such are the temptations, and such the facilities, to disobedience. It is useless, therefore, to advance further than to recommend this subject to the diligent attention of all the local governments, who will remember, that for the extermination of men who are exempt from the restraints both of Christianity and of civilization, there is no weapon so deadly or so certain as the produce of the distilleries.[21]

> On the subject of British law, and the punishment of crimes in overseas possessions, the Committee made some suggestions, not specifically for New South Wales, but concerning all British settlements.

20   It would be vain to expect the establishment of any other than a most imperfect system of justice amongst persons placed in such circumstances; but for the improvement of the present system some suggestions may be offered. Thus, when the British law is violated by the Aborigines within the British dominions, it seems right that the utmost indulgence compatible with a due regard for the lives and properties of others, should be shown for their ignorance and prejudices. Actions which they have been taught to regard as praiseworthy we consider as meriting the punishment of death. It is of course impossible to adopt or sanction the barbarous notions which have urged the criminal to the commission of the offence, but neither is it just to exclude them from our view in awarding the punishment of his crime.

[20] *ibid.*, pp. 75–6.
[21] *ibid.*, p. 78.

Again: in the case of offences committed beyond the borders, British subjects are amenable to colonial courts—the Aborigines are not. From this distinction arises, not merely a failure of justice, but, as far as our own people are concerned, an appearance at least of partiality and wrong, of which they are the victims. British subjects exposed to outrages in a country where there is no established form of civil government, and attacked by persons who are not amenable to our own courts, must be expected to resort to other means of self-defence, and not seldom to urge those means beyond the strict bounds of necessity or justice. It would, therefore, on every account, be desirable to induce the tribes in our vicinity to concur in devising some simple and effectual method of bringing to justice such of their own people as might be guilty of offences against the Queen's subjects.[22]

A later chapter will be devoted to British law and the Australian Aborigines.

Two years after the Report of the Select Committee appeared, it was still necessary for the Colonial Office to draw the attention of the Governor of New South Wales to the attitude and policies of the British Government.

21   You cannot over-rate the solicitude of H.M. Government on the subject of the Aborigines of New Holland. It is impossible to contemplate the condition and the prospects of that unfortunate race without the deepest commisseration. I am well aware of the many difficulties which oppose themselves to the effectual protection of these people, and especially of those which must originate from the exasperation of the Settlers on account of aggressions on their property, which are not the less irritating, because they are nothing else than the natural results of the pernicious examples held out to the aborigines, and of the many wrongs of which they have been the victims. Still it is impossible that the Government should forget that the original aggression was our own, and that we have never yet performed the sacred duty of making any systematic or considerable attempt to impart to the former occupiers of New South Wales the blessings of Christianity, or the knowledge of the Arts and advantages of civilised life. It is, I know, superfluous to stimulate your zeal in this service; yet I cannot be satisfied to quit the subject without commending it to your renewed attention. I am convinced that you may confidently reckon on the advice and co-operation of the Ministers of Religion of every Christian denomination, and you may calculate with the utmost confidence on the cordial support of the Crown in every well directed effort, for

[22] *ibid.*, p. 80.

securing to the Aboriginal Race of New Holland protection against injustice, and the enjoyment of every social advantage which our superior wealth and knowledge at once confer on us the power and impose on us the duty of imparting to them. For this purpose, you will use every effort to afford instruction to their Children and young men; you will seek out persons whose humanity leads them to be kind to the native races; and you will take means to reward the Missionaries who may engage in the good work.[23]

> The apparent failure of the system of Protectors (see Chapter 7) and of the various missions did not deter Lord Stanley from taking a positive attitude that something could yet be done.
> Shocked by the indifference and lightness with which atrocities against Aborigines were described in papers reaching England, he deplored the apparent want of feeling among the settlers. Lord Stanley emphasized the belief that all native peoples were capable of 'improvement'.

22   I cannot conclude this Despatch without expressing my sense of the importance of the subject of it, and my hope that your experience may enable you to suggest some general plan, by which we may acquit ourselves of the obligations which we owe towards this hapless race of beings. I should not without the most extreme reluctance admit that nothing can be done. That, with respect to them alone, the doctrines of Christianity must be inoperative, and the advantages of civilization incommunicable. I cannot acquiesce in the theory that they are incapable of improvement, and that their extinction, before the advance of the white settler, is a necessity which it is impossible to controul. I recommend them to your protection and favourable consideration with the greatest earnestness, but at the same time with perfect confidence; and I assure you that I shall be willing and anxious to co-operate with you in any arrangement for their Civilization, which may hold out a fair prospect of success.[24]

> The following chapters will examine the relationship between these official attitudes and the realities in New South Wales.

---

[23] Russell to Gipps, 21 December 1839, *H.R.A.*, I, xx, pp. 440–41.
[24] Stanley to Gipps, 20 December 1842, *ibid.*, xxii, p. 439.

2

The First Contacts

The British Government's attitude towards the Aborigines remained fairly consistent throughout the period under review, as has been shown in Chapter I; a number of government enquiries highlighted both the official attitude and the response of many colonists. Those colonists who came into close contact with the Aborigines revealed a variety of attitudes to them, and some of these are given below. Other parts of the chapter deal with the positive attempts made by individuals and by groups to 'conciliate their affections'.

Early observations on the Aborigines

The romantic concept of the Noble Savage—the native whose every want was supplied by nature, whose life was an example to materialistic Europeans—was echoed in an observation made by Captain Cook. This statement was the stronger for the contrast it made with Cook's normally matter-of-fact style of reporting his observations.

His views were probably shared by many of the early administrators and educated settlers.

23 From what I have said of the Natives of New Holland they may appear to some to be the most wretched People upon Earth; but in reality they are far more happier than we Europeans, being wholly unacquainted not only with the Superfluous, but with the necessary Conveniences so much sought after in Europe; they are happy in not knowing the use of them. They live in a Tranquility which is not disturbed by the Inequality of Condition. The Earth and Sea of their own accord furnishes them with all things necessary for Life. They covet not Magnificent Houses, Household-stuff etc.; they live in a Warm and fine Climate and enjoy a very wholsome Air, so that they have a very little need of Cloathing; and this they seem to be fully sencible of, for many to whom we gave Cloth etc., left it carelessly upon the Sea beach and in the Woods, as a thing they had no manner of use for; in short, they seem'd to set no Value upon anything we gave them, nor would they ever part with anything of their own for any one Article we could offer them. This in my opinion argues that they think themselves provided with all the necessarys of Life, and that they have no Superfluities. . . .[1]

The Aborigines' disregard for worldly goods was a major difficulty in later attempts made to 'civilize' them, for unlike other native peoples they did not value the goods white people offered — unless these took the form of tobacco or alcohol. Captain Watkin Tench saw the very nature of the Aborigines as the cause of the failure to implement Governor Phillip's orders:

24 . . . that greater progress in attaching them to us has not been made, I have only to regret; but that all ranks of men have tried to effect it, by every reasonable effort from which success might have been expected, I can testify; nor can I omit saying, that in the higher stations this has been eminently conspicuous. The public orders of Governor Phillip have invariably tended to promote such a behaviour on our side, as was most likely to produce this much wished-for event. To what cause then are we to attribute the distance which the accomplishment of it appears to be? I answer, to the fickle, jealous, wavering disposition of the people we have to deal with, who, like all other savages, are either too indolent, too indifferent, or too fearful to form an attachment on easy terms, with those who differ in habits and manners so widely from themselves.[2]

Within a short time, others came to see the natives as incredibly stupid creatures who needed to be taught to appreciate the superiority of the Europeans. The attitude revealed in the following extract is the more remarkable for its having been written by a missionary, William Pascoe Crook. Crook was writing to the Treasurer of the London Missionary Society.

25 One can scarcely walk 10 yards without meeting traces of the natives—their huts, which consist of a few branches of trees set up against a reclining tree or a piece of wood, but especially their fires. Perhaps the tenth part of the trees are partly burnt, yet no natives have been seen near this place. No one fears to venture into the woods, but I conceive it rather dangerous. We have nothing to fear from them here, as we are surrounded with sentinels, who challenge every one that comes near or within hearing after 9 o'clock, and if they cannot give the countersign sends them to the guard tent. When we first came into the harbour Capt. Mertho went with a few people into a lagoon that is in the north-west part of the harbour to examine it. Here, as they approached the shore,

---

[1] *Captain Cook's Journal during his Voyage* . . . in *H. M. Bark* Endeavour *1768–71*, London, 1893, p. 323.
[2] Watkin Tench, *A Narrative of the Expedition to Botany Bay*, third edition, London, 1789, p. 68.

they perceived a native on the beach with a shield and spear, branddishing his weapon as if to prevent their landing. A musket was fired over his head, when he ran, and was joined by others out of the bushes. They went off with amazing rapidity, kicking up the dust so that it appeared as if they were running thro' water. The party landed, went into a hut, where they found fire. They brought away a bark basket with them, and threw about the fire in such a manner that it communicated to the hut and burnt it. What impression this first visit made on the savages I leave you, sir, to judge. A party has been out twice for several days together, and have explored the whole harbour. They saw natives in several places, who were very familiar, but seemed to be amazing stupid. They knew not how to put a cup to their mouth, but when presented with any thing to drink would put their chin in the vessel; and when any thing was given them to eat they would open their mouths to receive it. None of their women has been seen. At one place they assembled in great numbers when the parties was separated, and alarmed them so that the other party arriving at the time were called on to fire, which they did, and wounded some and made them all fly. It was thought necessary to show them the effect of firearms; therefore one native, who had sat for some time under a tree, but who was following after the rest, was fired at by three persons at the same time and killed. The sailors stripped him, and brought away his ornaments and weapons.[3]

Nor did the Aborigines impress those Maoris who met them. Governor King reported on the visit to New South Wales of a Maori, Tip-a-he, and his son Tookey.

26 Of the natives of this country he had the most contemptible opinion, which both he and Tookey did not fail to manifest by discovering the utmost abhorrence at their going naked, and their want of ingenuity or inclination to procure food and make themselves comfortable, on which subject Tip-a-he on every occasion reproached them very severely. Their battles he treated as the most trifling mode of warfare, and was astonished that when they had their adversary down they did not kill him, which it seems is a custom among the New Zealanders and is carried to the most unrelenting pitch; indeed, no race of men could be treated with a more marked contempt than the natives of this country were by our visitors, who, it must be confessed, were infinitely their superiors in every respect.[4]

[3] W. Pascoe Crook to Joseph Hardcastle, 8 November 1803, *H.R.N.S.W.*, V, p. 256.
[4] King papers, The New Zealand Natives (n.d.), *H.R.N.S.W.*, VI, p. 7.

The picture that emerged with the passing years was one of increasing pessimism. There is no vestige of the Noble Savage in the four following extracts. George Clark wrote during his temporary charge of the Native Institution:

27   I have seen the miserable Africans first come from the holds of slave-ships; but they do not equal, in wretchedness and misery, the New Hollanders. They are the poorest objects on the habitable globe.[5]

The Rev. Daniel Tyerman and Mr George Bennet, the London Missionary Society visiting missionaries, recorded in their journal on 13 September 1824:

28   At Sydney, wither we returned on the 4th inst., we have this day seen a party of the natives, and surely there never trod on the face of this earth more abject creatures. Both men and women were in a state of absolute and shameless nudity, and several of them were stupidly intoxicated.[6]

The Rev. W. Yate, in giving evidence to the House of Commons 1835 Select Committee on Aborigines, revealed the colonial attitudes to the natives.

29   Must it not be acknowledged that the aborigines of Sydney have been treated as degraded creatures, unsusceptible of improvement, and hopelessly brutalized?—Yes, I think so. I have heard again and again people say that they were nothing better than dogs, and that it was no more harm to shoot them than it would be to shoot a dog when he barked at you.[7]

The Legislative Council Select Committee on the condition of the Aborigines in 1845 received evidence from the Lutheran missionary, the Rev. William Schmidt.

30   There is no doubt that they are the lowest in the scale of the human race, so far as they have come under my notice; they have no idea of a Divine Being; the impressions which we sometimes thought we had made upon them proved quite transient. Their faculties, especially their memories, are, in some instances, very good; but they appear to have no understanding of things which they commit to memory—I mean connected with religion.[8]

[5] George Clark, 1823. Reported in the *C.M.S. Missionary Register*, London, 1825, p. 100.
[6] Tyerman and Bennet, *Voyages and Travels . . . 1821–9*, London, 1840, p. 188.
[7] Evidence before the Select Committee on Aborigines (British Settlements) 1835, *B.P.P.*, Vol. VII, p. 202.
[8] *N.S.W.L.C.V.P.*, 1845, p. 20.

Observations on their mental capacity

Yet while these pessimistic observations were being made by some Europeans, there were others who saw that the Aborigines of New Holland were by no means lacking in intelligence. The Rev. Robert Cartwright was very optimistic about his projected work at the Native Institution at Parramatta:

31   ... I think it will now be admitted by every candid person, that the materials we have to work upon, although extremely rude, are nevertheless good. Buried as is the intellect of these savages in Augean filth, we may yet find gems of the first magnitude and brilliance.[9]

The Rev. James Günther was able to claim proofs of Aboriginal intellect.

32   Their intellectual faculties are by no means so inferior as is generally supposed; their mind is quite capable of culture; of this I have had many decisive proofs. At an average, they learn to read English, when young, as quickly as our own children, and those who have had much intercourse with the Aborigines have often been struck with the fact that at least the young men & boys very soon acquire and speak the English language correctly & fluently. You can draw out their minds so as to reflect & reason.[10]

One observer admitted that he had been surprised to find similarities between black and white, where he had expected to find differences:

33   ... notwithstanding many differences between the Black and the white man, their sympathies, likes and dislikes were very much what ours would have been if similarly situated; so that a very limited experience enabled both parties to understand and appreciate the position of the other. This fact only gradually dawned on me, as I had somehow started with the idea that I should find the Blacks as different from the white men in mind as they are in colour.[11]

The Rev. Dr J. D. Lang took the opportunity of an impending investigation by a committee of the House of Commons into the state of the Aboriginal inhabitants of the British empire to submit some written observations and comments. While asserting that, in general, the Australian Aborigines were abject in the extreme—degraded in mind and body—he added:

[9] Cartwright to Macquarie, 6 December 1819, *H.R.A.*, I, x, p. 264.
[10] James Günther, Lecture on the Aborigines of Australia, M.L. MSS.B505.
[11] Edward M. Curr, *Recollections of Squatting in Victoria* ... (From 1841 to 1851), [Melbourne 1833], Melbourne, 1965, pp. 52-3.

34 They are neither devoid of intelligence, however, nor destitute of capacity; and in their native wilds, and especially in seasons in which game is easily procurable, they are by no means strangers to a species of enjoyment. Their songs are artless, but agreeably melodious, and sometimes even poetical; their dances are an accurate imitation of the motions of the inferior animals that inhabit their native forests, and their mock fights are a still more accurate representation of real warfare than a European review. They seem to have no idea of a Supreme Creator and Governor of the Universe, and it would be difficult to determine whether they have any object of worship; but they believe in the existence of superior beings, both beneficent and malevolent; and in seasons of emergency they attempt to propitiate the former by lamentations and offerings of weapons of war, and to scare away the latter by brandishing their spears, and by other demonstrations of hostility. They have a superstitious dread of superior intelligences, but they have nothing that can properly be styled religious worship.[12]

> Their apparent ignorance of God and lack of any form of religious worship was an aspect of Aboriginal culture which most Europeans found totally incomprehensible. John Harper, investigating the possibility of establishing a mission station in the Bateman's Bay area on behalf of the Wesleyan Missionary Society, wrote in his Journal:

35 It must be acknowledged that, altho' these tribes are uncontaminated by the whites, yet, they are degraded as to Divine things, almost on a level with the brute. I could not find when speaking to my interpreter that they had any knowledge of a Supreme Being whatever. And in nothing, surely does the blinding and perverting influence of a vitiated heart, more strikingly appear, than in this failure among the Aborigines, of the knowledge of God. They are in a state of moral unfitness for heaven and its blessed and holy society: they are dying by hundreds and by thousands, and passing into eternity the unregenerate subjects of all their original and contracted pollutions, as completely unfit for heaven, and, as incapable of enjoying its society and its pleasures, as darkness is incapable of dwelling with light. While the Aborigines therefore perish, "it is without law".[13]

> A former Assistant Protector of Aborigines found it difficult to reconcile their apparent intelligence with their spiritual degradation.

36 Whilst the undoubted proofs of mental superiority displayed amongst them, in the usual varieties which characterise com-

---

[12] Lang to T. F. Buxton, 10 June 1834, in evidence to Select Committee on Aborigines (British Settlements), *B.P.P.*, Vol. VII, p. 682.
[13] Bonwick Transcripts, Box 53, M.L.

munities of the human species, demand for them the rank which their Creator designed them to occupy amongst rational intelligences—the awful predominance amongst them of sins of the most obscene and revolting description, alike destructive to the body and to the soul, demonstrates that they are without God in the world. They seem indeed so far removed from original righteousness, so entirely lost to all moral and spiritual perception, as to render it doubtful, in the estimation of those who have had the best opportunities of judging, whether there exists amongst them any notions of the existence of a Supreme being, which contain the slightest analogy to natural and revealed truth.[14]

> Edward Curr sought to explain the widespread notion that Aborigines believed only in the devil.

37   Religious worship the Bangerang had none. As the result of several conversations on such subjects, the conclusion to which I came was, that they stood in considerable awe of a powerful spiritual being, whose interference in their affairs was usually of a malevolent character, but whose principal attributes (such as power, knowledge &c) we Christians attribute to God. This spirit the whites had taught the Blacks to call *debble-debble* (the devil), and hence people commonly say the Blacks believe in the devil, but not in God.[15]

Early views on prospects of civilizing the natives

> With such views of the Aborigines prevailing it is not surprising that many white people expressed doubts that any attempts to civilize them would be difficult, if not impossible. As early as 1817 one missionary had concluded that the effort was scarcely worth while.

38   There does not appear to be the least encouragement to attempt a civilization of them. In the first place they are but few in number. There is not to be found 500 in as many miles. These tribes are very small. The largest I have seen contained only twelve.— Their language is quite different in the pronunciation. They are afraid to travel out of their own Boundaries—will attend to nothing without a reward and as soon as it be given they cease to act.[16]

> Others were more optimistic. The Rev. William Walker believed a civilizing project would be successful though slow.

39   I met with great numbers of natives, that excited considerable interest in my heart. The men are strong, active, and

---

[14] James Dredge, *Brief Notices of the Aborigines of New South Wales*, Geelong, 1845, p. 11.
[15] Edward Curr, *op. cit.*, p. 129.
[16] S. Leigh to Dr A. Clarke, 14 October 1817, Bonwick Transcripts, Box 50, M.L.

generally robust; the females cheerful, pleasantly featured, but dimunitive in stature; and the children are lively, interesting, and present some hopeful ground to cultivate: but all are excessively idle and vagrant.

The more I see of the disposition and habits of the New Hollander, the more rigidly am I confirmed in the opinion, that a great length of time must elapse before any extensive good will be effected. And that is not with the adults, but with young men, and children that the great work must be commenced, and through them the saving plan of redemption be disseminated to the uttermost bounds of their scattered, uncivilised, unsocial, and cannibal tribes. Traversing the woods in their tribes, and living in a kind of domesticated manner with them will never do the work, nor will it prove conducive to their more quickly and readily receiving the blessed and saving truths of religion.[17]

This idea of concentrating on the young Aborigines was frequently put forward as the most likely way to succeed. Peter Cunningham had a strong argument for securing the children.

40 A degree of force we find to be absolutely necessary to urge man toward civilisation, in his primitive debased state, and cause him to break up those habits he had acquired. It is only when the mind is more enlightened, and reason supersedes animal instinct, that civilisation will steadily advance among the community by the exertions of individual members. In countries, therefore, where absolute hereditary chiefs exist, you have only to gain *them* over to forward your views; but in countries differently circumstanced you must absolutely *secure* the young, wean them from parental influence, and infuse into them new ideas and opinions before you can make much progress.[18]

One unusual objection to any organized attempts to 'civilize' the Aborigines came from Samuel Marsden.

41 The Revd. Mr. Marsden, whose mind is prepossed [*sic*] in favour of the New Zealanders, has indeed very little hope concerning the Inhabitants of this Country. We spoke with him about them, he started several objections, the last of which was that they eat snakes. As however the New Zealanders eat men, and have yet proved

---

[17] William Walker to General Secretaries of Wesleyan Missionary Society, *ibid.*, Box 53, M.L.
[18] Peter Cunningham, *Two Years in New South Wales*, third edition, London, 1828, Vol. II, p. 44.

capable of receiving Christianity; I entertain also no doubt with regard to the Aborigines, who eat snakes.[19]

First attempts to 'civilize' the natives

A little over a year after his arrival in New South Wales, the first chaplain, the Rev. Richard Johnson, took an Aboriginal girl into his household. He wrote to Henry Fricker about this experiment.

42 Have a native girl under my care. Have had her now about 11 months. ... Have taken some pains with Abaroo (about 15 years old) to instruct her in reading, & have no reason to complain of her improvement. She can likewise begin to speak a little English & is useful in several things about our little Hutt. Have taught her the Lord's Prayer &C., and as she comes better to understand me, endeavour to instruct her respecting a Supreme Being, &c. Wish to see these poor heathen brought to the knowledge of Xtianity & hope in time to see or hear of the dawnings of that time when these shall be given for our Lord's heritage, & the uttermost parts of the earth for his Possession.[20]

Alas for Johnson's optimism, only a few months after he wrote this letter, Abaroo absconded.

43 The wife of the Chaplain adopted her into the family and trained her in European habits and faith. But, after eighteen months, the girl blushed into womanhood and sought a more natural protector, with whom she fled to the bush.[21]

Marsden, too, began on an optimistic note, by adopting a native child.

44 My native boy, whom I have had now more than four years improves much; he is become useful in the family; can speak the English language very well; and has begun to read.[22]

But from the beginning, the great difficulties involved in trying to 'civilize' the Aborigines in the midst of a penal settlement were only too apparent. Johnson sought to remedy this by such arguments as those contained in An Address to the Inhabitants of the Colonies established in New South Wales and Norfolk Island, which he presented in 1792.

---

[19] J. S. C. Handt to Church Missionary Society, 30 September 1831, Church Missionary Society microfilmed archives relating to the Australian and New Zealand Mission 1808–84, London, 1959.
[20] Johnson to Henry Fricker, 9 April 1790. Quoted in G. Mackaness, ed., *Some Letters of Rev. Richard Johnson B.A.*, Sydney, 1954, Part I, p. 29.
[21] James Bonwick, *First Twenty Years of Australia*, Melbourne and Sydney, 1882, p. 180.
[22] Marsden to William Wilberforce, 1799, Bonwick Transcripts, Box 49, M.L.

45 He sought to shame them into propriety by showing the effect of their conduct upon the heathen savages of New Holland. "If these ignorant natives," wrote he, "as they become more and more acquainted with our language and manners, hear you, many of you, curse, swear, lie, abound in every kind of obscene and profane conversation; and if they observe that it is common with you to steal, to break the Sabbath, to be guilty of uncleanness, drunkenness, and other abominations, how must their minds become prejudiced, and their hearts hardened, against that pure and holy religion which *we* profess!"[23]

> In spite of such exhortations throughout the succeeding years, hostility between the two races grew as the colony grew. It was this hostility that led Governor Macquarie to investigate ways in which more friendly relations could be developed, and with this end in mind he established the Native Institution in 1814.

46 From Whatever Motives or Causes Some of these Natives have been Induced to Commit Acts of Hostility against the Settlers, it seems to bear a reasonable Inference that Provocation or Aggression from some Undiscovered or Unacknowledged Cause may have given Rise to them, Under an Impression of temporary Revenge; but when once Induced to forego this Vindictive Spirit, which Kindness and Encouragement and Social Intercourses together Would Sooner or later bring about, their next Step towards Civilization would be rapid and easy, and they Would learn to Appreciate that Degree of Importance to Which they had thus progressively Attained.

From Considerations of this kind, Which in a great Measure have been Guided and Strengthened by My own personal Knowledge and Observation, I have determined to make an Experiment towards the Civilization of these Natives, Which is the Object I have in View by this Address, and trust it Will Meet Your Lordship's benevolent Patronage. As a preliminary Measure I intend to establish an Institution at Parramatta, first on a Small Scale under the Direction of a Mr. William Shelly (formerly a Missionary), Whom I shall Appoint as Superintendent for Educating, and bringing up to Habits of Industry and Decency, the Youth of both Sexes, Commencing at the Outset with Six Boys and Six Girls. Mr. Shelley Appears to be Well Qualified for such an Undertaking, is a Moral, Well Meaning Man, and has Manifested great Zeal and Promptitude On this Occasion, Insomuch that I Consider him a very fit Person to be Entrusted for such a Purpose.[24]

---

[23] James Bonwick, *op. cit.*, p. 221.
[24] Macquarie to Bathurst, 8 October 1814, *H.R.A.*, I, viii, p. 369.

Mr Shelley was enthusiastic about the prospects of the establishment:

47   ... about five months past I stated in a short address to His Excellency Governor Macquarie my Ideas on the practicability of civilizing the Natives of this Territory—he was pleased to express his approbation & requested me to draw up a plan for an Institution and make out an estimate of the maintenance of a certain number of children, this I did and His Excellency has forwarded them to His Majesties Ministers for approval. In the mean time the Governor has been pleased to appoint me Manager of the Institution. A house is purchased and a large piece of ground is enclosing for the accommodation of the children. I have had several children for some time and find them remarkably tractable. They have a peculiar aptness in learning the English language and pronounce it with much propriety. From the rambling Naked state of these poor Natives they have generally been supposed as incapable of improvement but I am persuaded that under the blessing of God they are as capable of instruction as any other untutored savages.[25]

Commissioner J. T. Bigge, in the second of his three Reports, recorded the attitude of Marsden to Macquarie's efforts to civilize the Aborigines.

48   Previous to the formation of this society, Governor Macquarrie had proposed to Mr. Marsden to form another, for the civilization of the native black inhabitants of New South Wales. Mr. Marsden, though not averse to this proposition, stated to Governor Macquarrie, that from his observation of the character of the black native, he had great doubts of the success of any scheme of civilization in weaning them from their natural habits, or subduing their aversion to restraint. He, however, suggested, that if any attempt was to be made, the best prospects of success would be afforded by instructing the younger natives in common agricultural operations, and making them sensible of the benefits immediately derivable from the cultivation of the earth.[26]

In fact, one of Macquarie's experiments *was* to encourage natives to settle on the land and become agriculturalists.

49   I have it Also in Contemplation to Allot a piece of Land in Port Jackson bordering on the Sea Shore *for a few of the Adult Natives*, Who have promised to Settle there and Cultivate the Ground. Such an Example Cannot, I think, fail of Inviting and Encouraging other Natives to Settle on and Cultivate Lands, preferring the productive

---

[25] Shelley to Rev. G. Burder, 6 October 1814, Bonwick Transcripts, Box 49, M.L.
[26] J. T. Bigge, *Report of the Commissioner of Inquiry on the Judicial Establishments of New South Wales and Van Diemen's Land*, 1823, pp. 27–8.

Effects of their own Labor and Industry to the Wild and precarious Pursuits of the Woods.[27]

> In the following March Macquarie was able to report to Earl Bathurst that sixteen adult natives had settled on a small farm with their families.[28] However, the experiment did not fulfil Macquarie's hopes.

50 On *31 January 1815* an attempt was made to induce a number of the *adult Blacks* to locate and settle themselves at "George's Head". There were Huts erected, and small patches of Garden Ground were prepared for them; Rations and Clothing were provided for them, and a Boat was given to them. A European man was appointed to assist the Natives but this plan was not attended with success. But the European, feeling little, if any, interest in the welfare of the Natives, did not protect the property thus appropriated for them, and in a short period the Huts and Gardens, &c were destroyed, and the Boat was lost; and this attempt failed.[29]

> In spite of the premature death of William Shelley, early reports of the Native Institution were highly encouraging.

51 With respect to the capacity of the Natives to learning, we can have no doubt, as the Native Institution founded by Govt about 3 years ago under the Superintendency of our late much lamented Mr. Wm. Shelley fully proves. There are now 17 children in the Native School & under the management of the widow Shelley—the greater part of these poor native children can read their Testament or Bible, and lately a part of them are admitted into the Sunday Schools.[30]

> In the following year the children from the Institution were taken to the annual feast given by Governor Macquarie to the Aborigines at Parramatta. About one hundred and fifty natives were present, and the children were examined before their parents and the assembled company.

52 The Committee then proceeded to examine the children of both sexes (16 in number), and were highly gratified with their progress in reading and writing, and particularly with the attention the little females paid to their needle-work;—thus bringing to the expanded mind of the Philanthropist and the Christian the peculiar advantages of an Institution founded on such liberal and praiseworthy principles.[31]

---

[27] Macquarie to Bathurst, 8 October 1814, *H.R.A.*, I, viii, pp. 369–70.
[28] Macquarie to Bathurst, 24 March 1815, *ibid.*, p. 467.
[29] William Cowper to W. W. Burton, 11 June 1838, *Papers relating to Aborigines 1796–1819* MS. no. A1161, M.L.
[30] Rowland Hassall to Rev. G. Burder; 1 April 1817, Bonwick Transcripts, Box 50, M.L.
[31] *Sydney Gazette*, 3 January 1818.

In 1819 about twenty children from the Native Institution met almost a hundred white children from European schools at the Anniversary School Examination.

53 Prizes were prepared for distribution among such as should be found to excel in the early rudiments of education, moral and religious; and it is not less strange than pleasing to remark, in answer to an erroneous opinion which had long prevailed with many, namely, that the Aborigines of this country were insusceptible to any mental improvement which could adapt them to the purposes of civilized association, that a black girl of fourteen years of age, between three and four years in the school, bore away the chief prize, with much satisfaction to their worthy adjudgers and auditors.[32]

Macquarie's delight in telling the Colonial Office was understandable.

54 I have much pleasure in reporting to Your Lordship that the Institution, established by Me some few Years since at Parramatta for the Support and Instruction of the Children of the Ab-Origines of the Colony, has succeeded far beyond my most sanguine Expectations, the Children having made very great Progress in all those Useful and Necessary Branches of Instruction they are taught, evincing good Natural Understandings, and an Aptitude for learning whatever is proposed to be taught them. There are now Eighteen healthy Boys and Girls in this Institution, well Clothed, well-fed and well instructed in the Common Branches of Education, Including Needle Work for the Girls, and Knowledge of Agriculture for the Boys, there being a large Field and Garden attached to the School House for them to work in. Nothing has yet been done in this Colony that has so much Conciliated the Adult Natives to the Interests of the British Government generally, as the Establishment of this Institution, as they appear to be highly gratified and delighted beyond description with the Contented and happy Appearance of their Children.

The Adults now regularly attend the Annual Meeting of the Natives at Parramatta on the 28th of December of each Year, on which occasion the Children at the Institution are paraded in presence of their Parents, read before them, and produce Specimens of their Progress in Education.[33]

> The *Sydney Gazette*, in reporting the 1820 Parramatta gathering, looked to the prospects such progress opened up:

[32] *ibid.*, 17 February 1819.
[33] Macquarie to Bathurst, 24 March 1819, *H.R.A.*, I, x, p. 95.

55   . . . every heart must have fondly dilated with the glorious and humanizing conception of beholding so many, at least, snatched from the wilds of barbarism, ignorance, and misery. To every reflecting mind, the benignancy of the Institution must *then* have shone forth with all the resplendency so vast and glorious an object is capable of emitting and embracing; viz. the civilization and salvation of thousands of fellow creatures, at present involved in gross darkness; —but, we heartily rejoice in having it in our power to declare, that a CORNER STONE is being laid, which will inevitably (by the Divine Blessing) become so permanent that future ages will be enabled to raise the fairest structures upon the solidity of its foundation. . .[34]

It was perhaps to be expected that the example of the Native Institution would lead other groups to consider the possibility of undertaking projects to 'civilize' the Aborigines. The Wesleyans, many of whose missionaries were residing in New South Wales, were in a good position to begin activities.

56   I think the best plan to do them any permanent good would be to Set apart a pious & judicious School Master to instruct them in reading (which they would be very soon taught) and Government be applied to for a grant of Land (2 or 3000 acres) on which wheat and vegetables might be raised for the support of teachers & as an inducement for the natives to collect themselves together as at one common centre—this Measure would at once cure them of those vagrant habits in which they now live and give their teachers an opportunity of instructing them (they must have a stimulus or they wou^d not attend) I have not the least doubt but Govt would immediately accede to a proposal of the kind, I will see Governor Macquarie on the subject before long, and if His Excellency thinks proper will request him to write to the Secretary of State specifically on these points, perhaps the Missionaries or more properly School Masters might be victualled from His Majesty's Stores which would greatly relieve the Mission fund, . . . I am very solicitous that the Wesleyans should have the honor of restoring some of the Pagans in these extensive Seas.[35]

In August 1819 a handful of leading citizens formed the New South Wales Society for Promoting Christian Knowledge amongst the Aborigines of New South Wales and its Dependencies. Subscribers could become members for £1 per annum, or life members for £10.

---

[34] *Sydney Gazette*, 30 December 1820.
[35] Rev. W. Lawry to Wesleyan Missionary Society, 15 July 1819, Bonwick Transcripts, Box 50, M.L.

57   We, the undersigned, duly considering and highly appreciating the great Advantages of Civilization & the very exalted Privileges and inestimable Benefits of Christianity, which in its benign influence we ourselves enjoy under an enlightened and happy Constitution, do most tenderly commiserate the low and wretched condition of our heathen Brethren in these Parts of the world. We feel that, as an important and indispensable Duty, it is incumbent on us, by every pious and conciliatory means, to recommend to the Aborigines of New South Wales the Habits of useful Industry and Civilization; and more especially to lead them to an acquaintance with the first Principles of the Christian Religion.[36]

The signatories were James Erskine, Lieutenant Governor; John Wylde, Judge Advocate N.S.W.; Barron Field, Judge of the Supreme Court; William Cowper, Assistant Chaplain; Richard Hill, Assistant Chaplain. The Society was approved by Governor Macquarie who became its Patron.
   The Rev. Robert Cartwright put forward ideas for extending the benefits derived from the Native Institution. Governor Macquarie was sufficiently impressed with Cartwright's plans to forward them to Earl Bathurst.

58   The Subject of the *Native Institution*, Some Years since established by Me at Parramatta, which has excited a very Considerable Interest generally on its behalf, as well from the principle of Humanity, which first gave Rise to it, as also from the Degree of Success with which it has been heretofore attended, having also particularly Attracted the Attention of the Reverend Mr. Cartwright one of the Colonial Chaplains, who is a most exemplary and benevolent Man, He has turned his thoughts Seriously towards the Means of ameliorating the Situation of the Natives and of Conveying Education and Habits of Industry to the Young of both sexes among them, by extending the Scale of Benefit and Improvement derivable from the present Institution; and for this worthy purpose has lately furnished me with the Prospectus of Such a Plan for a Native Establishment as he deems adequate to the Contemplated Objects.
   Having perused Mr. Cartwright's Plan with Much Attention, I am inclined not only to Yield him the highest praise for the Zeal which has actuated him on the occasion, but, feeling also fully satisfied with the Justness of his Hints and Observations, have been led so far to Approve of it, as to Sanction it being Carried at an early day into Effect.
   I do myself the Honor to transmit Your Lordship herewith Copies of the Letters, addressed to me on this humane Subject by Mr.

---

[36] Bonwick Transcripts, Box 50, M.L.

Cartwright, which I trust will Induce Your Lordship also to Sanction and approve of the proposed Establishment on the Grounds urged by Mr. Cartwright.

The rapid Increase of British Population, and the Consequent Occupancy of the Lands formerly dwelt on by the Natives having driven these harmless Creatures to more remote Situations, It is my purpose to form the proposed Establishment in the distant fertile Tract of Country, lately discovered by Mr. Throsby, which will bring it nearer to their present place of Inhabitation and at the same time render it less subject to be disturbed by Vagrants, than if it were placed in the Settled Districts; and it will have a further Advantage from the Circumstance of the Lands in this new Country not being appropriated, whereby I will be enabled to Assign a Suitable portion of Land for the Necessary Buildings and the great Object of Cultivation in which these Natives are to be Instructed.

For the purpose of Erecting a Village, and holding out ample Encouragement to the Industry of the Natives, who are expected to enter into the Institution, I propose to Assign a proportion of Land to the Extent of ten thousand Acres for their permanent Benefit; and I beg to express the Confident Hope that Your Lordship will Approve of this Measure, as One worthy of British Feelings to a harmless Race, who have been without Struggle driven by the Progress of British Industry from their ancient places of Inhabitation.[37]

Mr Cartwright predicted that his proposed institution would be beneficial not only to the Aborigines but to the whole Colony.

59   As the hope of honor and reward is a most powerful incentive to industry and improvement, it would certainly tend to promote the interest of the Institution, as well as the Benefit of the whole Colony, if such Establishment were formed at no great distance from our Settlement. For I will venture to predict that the time is not far distant when, at our public annual Exhibition, these sable Australians will enter the lists with our more highly favored Albion's Sons and bear away the prize of merit.

As it would be matter of no small Entertainment and profit, I shall be anxious to produce every Year, not only good readers and writers, and those who can give a reasonable and scriptural account of their Faith and practise in religious matters, But also those who are well skilled in every branch of economy.

This Colony I am persuaded, would not only experience relief in the disappearing of those Companies of black savage beggars, which

---

[37] Macquarie to Bathurst, 24 February 1820, *H.R.A.*, I, x, pp. 262-3.

are likely to become a pest in Town and Country, but would find a protection and powerful Ally in such an Establishment, and, I may add, an example to be admired and imitated.[38]

> Commissioner Bigge's account of the Native Institution with its precise facts and figures contrasts vividly with the ornate language of the *Sydney Gazette* (Doc. 55) and his caution with regard to the long-term effects of the school was to be justified:

60   ... it appears that thirty-seven boys and twenty-seven girls have been placed in it, and of these, six have absconded, two have died, and one was taken by his father to reside upon some land that was given to him. These children have been taught to read and write, and have been instructed in the principles of the Christian religion. They also attend church regularly at Parramatta, and join in the service. The girls have been taught the common sorts of needle-work and domestic service, and two have been hired out as servants to respectable inhabitants of the country.

From the experiment that has been made at this establishment, no doubt can be entertained of the natural capacities of the native black children, and their power of attaining the means of improving their condition. It yet remains to be proved, whether the habits they acquire in the schools are permanent.

. . .

By one of the returns that was furnished by the Rev. Mr. Hill, who is now secretary to the several institutions that I have mentioned, the annual expense of the maintenance, instruction and clothing of each of the native black children amounts to the sum of 15L. 13s.[39]

> After the arrival of Governor Darling who, as we have seen, was instructed to seek advice from the Archdeacon concerning the conversion of the Aborigines to Christianity, the Church of England became more closely involved in the task. The Archdeacon wrote:

61   In the mean time, I proposed to the Trustees that a separate School should be formed in some part, not too distant, but at the same time quite apart from any Town, at which such Children as could be got should be placed. This was fixed at a place called Black Town, about 14 Miles N.W. of Parramatta, and a Person named Hall with his Wife, well qualified for the undertaking, were placed there to conduct the Establishment. I caused such Black Children, as were in the Male and Female Orphan Institutions, to

---

[38] Cartwright to Macquarie, 18 January 1820, *ibid.*, p. 270.
[39] J. T. Bigge, *Report of the Commissioner of Inquiry on the state of Agriculture and Trade in the Colony of New South Wales*, 1823, p. 73.

be removed there, and directed Mr. Hall to continue the Common Elements of Education, in which they had been previously instructed, but at the same time to devote a large portion of their time to work, the Boys to be taught Carpentering (he having been bred up to that Trade) and the Girls plain Needle work by his Wife. Mr. Hall having a very religious turn of mind, I directed him to give these Children religious Instruction, and at the same time to Read the Church Service and short plain Discourses on the Sunday to the Parties of Convicts employed on the Roads in that Neighbourhood, and thus uniting with his other occupation a very important matter in this Colony.

The time has been too short to pronounce decisively on this experiment; but, as the Trade of a Carpenter is cleanly, useful, and capable of being carried on in a Shed under the Eye of the Master, I preferred it to any other as the best calculated to Civilize them, and destroy their erratic Habits, which are so strongly implanted in them that, until these are got under, little hope of success can be expected. One of these Boys aged 17, who had been bred up at the Male Orphan School, was apprenticed to a most respectable Person in Sydney, Mr. Thorp, Assistant Engineer to the Government, to learn the Trade of a Builder. After remaining about 10 days, I regret to say the Boy ran away into the Woods, and, although the Police has been Searching for him, no intelligence has as yet been received of him.[40]

> The Archdeacon's instructions to Mr Hall are most revealing of the European attitudes to 'civilizing' the Aborigines. The white man's belief in order and industry was to be imposed upon the native children.

62 I beg to inform you that His Excellency the Governor has approved of your being placed at Black Town together with your Wife to take charge of that Establt. for the civilization of the Black Natives both Male and Female and also to give Catechetical Instruction to the Prisoners of the Crown in that Vicinity. . . .

With regard to the Children the object in view must be instruction in reading writing and the common rules of cyphering and the common operations of labour—but especially to teach the Boys the trade of a Carpenter. The Girls should be taught plain needle work and spinning especially from the down of the opossum which you might employ the parents of the Children to collect giving them small presents of tea sugar or flour in return and of which a separate account should be kept.

When this is spun both boys and girls may be taught to knit stockings or other articles.

[40] Scott to Darling, 27 March 1828, *H.R.A.*, I, xiv, pp. 56–7.

I would recommend the following rules to be observed subject to such deviation only as may be found absolutely necessary.
1. The Children to be up and dressed by 6. and set to work.
2. To wash themselves at 1/2 past 7 go to Prayers and Breakfast at 8.
3. To work till 10 Clock.
4. To wash and go to school from 10 till 12 write one Copy read half an hour cypher 1 Hour.
5. To dine at 1/4 after 12 and play till 1.
6. To School at 1 read & cypher till 2.
7. To work from 2 till 6 the boys at carpentering the girls sewing and knitting.
8. To play and wash and be ready for supper at 7.
9. To Prayers at 1/2 past 7 and to be in bed at 8.
10. On Saturday morning to be devoted to instruction of Church Service.
11. The following rewards to be given in Tickets for
    1 Good Behaviour
    2 Good Work
    3 Religious knowledge in which they are to be examined every Sunday of one Ticket at each time at the discretion of the master and mistress and for every 10 Tickets an account shall be kept in a book entitling the children to sixpence to be laid out for their benefit at the discretion of the Visitor.

The rations for one week are to be for each child
7 lbs of Maize Meal. 3 1/2 lbs Beef or mutton, 5 lbs of flour, 2 ozs of Tea 1 lb of Sugar 2 oz Soap 7 pints of rice or maize flour for soup 2 suits of Slop clothing in a year to be delivered on the 1st of Janry, and 1st of July.

The meals are to consist at Breakfast of 1 quart of Maize meal sugar and milk each for dinner Beef Soup with the meat with rice or meal vegetables and for Supper Bread and Tea.

You will be allowed for yourself Wife and three children 21 lbs of meat 21 lbs of Bread or flour 3 lbs of Sugar 8 oz tea and 1 Bus of Maize for a Horse weekly to be accounted for with the other rations & a Salary of £100 Stg. per ann. to be pd. quarterly.[41]

> The concept of fitting the Aborigines into the work force was prevalent throughout the period, though not all Europeans believed them capable of learning a trade, or thought it necessary to use them as anything but unskilled labourers, and servants.

63 Particular notice was taken of two aboriginal native boys and a girl who were brought up in the house of the Rev. W. WALKER

---

[41] Scott to Hall, 6 February 1827, Scott Letter Book No. 1, MS. no. A850, M.L.

at Parramatta, and accompanied him to the meeting. These children have made a very creditable progress in reading and writing, and are excellent house servants—a proof that the intellect of the natives is not so debased as to be incapable of cultivation if judicious measures be adopted.[42]

> Cunningham found that the natives throughout the County of Cumberland had become so dependent upon the whites that if they could not beg or steal, they frequently found employment. The natives were not unaware of being exploited.

64   Many of these men work upon the settlers' farms at odd jobs throughout the year, and also at harvest of late. Indeed it seems probable that, with proper encouragement and good treatment, numbers of the more civilised natives may turn out useful members of society. A gentleman of Mulgoa, bordering on the Blue mountains, had, in 1826, thirty acres of wheat reaped by a party of them in fourteen days as well as by whites. They were always out before the whites in the morning, and were fed and paid a regular price for their labour, the gentleman giving it as his opinion, that the chief cause of dislike to work on the part of the Cumberland blacks is their being cheated by the small convict settlers.[43]

> One of the most revealing summaries of these early attempts to conciliate the affections of the Aborigines was made by Mrs Shelley, who ran the Native Institution for about eight years after her husband's death. Giving evidence before the Committee on the Aborigines question in 1838 she said:

65   I found their dispositions and their capacity for learning to vary very much. Some of them read and wrote well, and understood arithmetic to a certain extent; but, I always found the half-caste children quicker and more tractable than the blacks. All who were old enough, were taught their Catechism, which they repeated very accurately,—and they were taken regularly to Church.

. . .

I visited the settlement two or three times during Mr. Walker's charge, and found a great many of the old blacks amongst them, and that they were in consequence in a very unsettled state.

. . .

Since that period, some of them have occasionally visited me, and I found they had relapsed into all the bad habits of the untaught natives. A few of the boys went to sea, but I have not heard what has become of them. Most of the girls have turned out very bad, but

---

[42] *Sydney Gazette*, 9 January 1830.
[43] Peter Cunningham, *op. cit.*, Vol. II, pp. 6–7.

there is one exception in a half-caste girl, who was married to a white man, and was very industrious, taking in needlework, &c. I have not, however, heard of her for two years.

I have frequently conversed with them since, on religious subjects, but they turned them into laughter, and said they had forgotten about it.[44]

The observation made by Tyerman and Bennet painted what they saw as a most discouraging picture.

66 All attempts to civilize the savage occupants have been fruitless; it must be confessed, however, that those attempts have been few and feeble.[45]

---

[44] Report from the Committee on the Aborigines Question, *N.S.W.L.C.V.P.*, 1838, pp. 54–5.
[45] Tyerman and Bennet, *op. cit.*, p. 187.

3
Breakdown of Official Policy

Early clashes

In spite of the government instructions 'to live in amity and kindness' with the Aborigines, trouble between them and the Europeans occurred almost immediately. Governor Phillip showed himself to be most anxious to avoid clashes, and to understand the Aborigines and their problems—problems usually caused by the effects of the European invasion on the Natives' food supplies.

67   Yesterday twenty of the natives came down to the beach, each armed with a number of spears, and seized on a good part of the fish caught in the seine. The coxswain had been ordered, however small the quantity he caught, always to give them a part whenever any of them came where he was fishing, and this was the first time they ever attempted to take any by force. While the greatest number were seizing the fish, several stood at a small distance with their spears poised ready to throw them if any resistance had been made, but the coxswain very prudently permitted them to take what they chose, and parted good friends. They, at present, find it very difficult to support themselves.

In consequence of what happened yesterday, no boat will in future go down to the harbour without an officer.[1]

Phillip saw quite clearly that the white men were largely responsible. Equally clearly the Aborigines saw the whole of the European community as blameworthy and took revenge as opportunity offered.

68   It is still a doubt whether the cattle we lost have been killed by the natives, or if they have strayed into the country. I fear the former, and am sorry to say that the natives now attack any straggler they meet unarmed; and though the strictest orders have been given to keep the convicts within bounds, neither the fear of death or punishment prevents their going out in the night; and one

---

[1] Phillip to Nepean, 10 July 1788 *H.R.A.*, I, i, pp. 66–7.

has been killed since the Sirius sailed. The natives, who appear strictly honest amongst themselves, leave their fizgigs, spears, &c., on the beach, or in their huts, when they go a-fishing; these articles have been taken from them by the convicts, and the people belonging to the transports buy them at the risk of being prosecuted as receivers of stolen goods, if discovered. The natives, as I have observed, revenge themselves on any they meet unarmed; it is not possible to punish them without punishing the innocent with the guilty, and our own people have been the aggressors.

The natives still refuse to come amongst us, and those who are supposed to have murthered several of the convicts have removed from Botany Bay, where they have always been more troublesome than in any other part. I now doubt whether it will be possible to get any of those people to remain with us, in order to get their language, without using force; they see no advantage that can arise from us that may make amends for the loss of that part of the harbour in which we occasionally employ the boats in fishing.[2]

Paterson was torn between the ideal of living peacefully with the Aborigines, and the realities of the need to develop agricultural settlements further afield from Sydney.

69 The number of settlers on the banks of the Hawkesbury, with their families, amounts to upwards of four hundred persons, and their grounds extend near thirty miles along the banks on both sides of the river. They have for some time past been annoyed by the natives, who have assembled in large parties for the purpose of plundering them of their corn; and from the impossibility of furnishing each settler with firearms for his defence, several accidents have happened. Within a few weeks five people have been killed and several wounded. It therefore became absolutely necessary to take some measures which might secure to the settlers the peaceable possession of their estates, and without which, from the alarm these murders have created, I very much feared they would have abandoned the settlement entirely, and given up the most fertile spot which has yet been discovered in the colony. I therefore sent a detachment of two subalterns and sixty privates of the New South Wales Corps to the river, as well to drive the natives to a distance, as for the protection of the settlers. With this view a subaltern's party is to remain there after the service they are now gone upon is performed.

I have just received a report from the commanding officer of the detachment informing me that the night after his arrival at the river

---

[2] Phillip to Sydney, 30 October 1788, *ibid.*, p. 96.

the party had fired upon and pursued a large body of natives, who had concealed themselves in the neighbouring woods during the day, and at night came to a settler's farm to plunder it; that he supposes seven or eight natives were killed, and that he was taking every measure he thought likely to deter them from appearing there again.

I have now in my possession one man and four women (natives) who were taken prisoners some short time since at the Hawkesbury from amongst a large party who were plundering the settlers. I mean to keep them until they can be made to understand that it is not their interest to do us injuries, and that we are readier to be friends than enemies; but that we cannot suffer our people to be inhumanly butchered, and their labour rendered useless by their depredations, with impunity.

It gives me concern to have been forced to destroy any of these people, particularly as I have no doubt of their having been cruelly treated by some of the first settlers who went out there; however, had I not taken this step, every prospect of advantage which the colony may expect to derive from a settlement formed on the banks of so fine a river as the Hawkesbury would be at an end.[3]

> Orders were given to the small farmers in outlying settlements to form groups to resist native attacks. Absconding convicts who joined the Aborigines added to the difficulties.

70 The frequent attacks and depredations to which the settlers situated on the banks of the Hawkesbury and other places are liable from the natives renders it indispensably necessary for the general security of the farmers and their families, as well as for the preservation of their crops, that they should upon all occasions of alarm mutually afford their assistance to each other by assembling without a moment delay whenever any numerous body of the natives are known to be lurking about the farms. By such an active attention to their own safety and interest there can be no doubts but that the visits of those people would be less frequent than of late they have been, and many lives would thereby be preserved.

It is therefore hereby expected and ordered by the Governor that all the people residing in the different districts of the settlement, whether the alarm be on their own farms or any other person's, do upon such occasions shew the most scrupulous attention to this direction, in order that those frequent murders and robberies may be prevented. If it shall hereafter be known that any settler or other person do withdraw or keep back their assistance from those who may be threatened or in danger of being attack'd, they will be

---

[3] Paterson to Dundas, 15 June 1795, *ibid.*, iii, pp. 499–500.

proceeded against as persons disobeying the rules and orders of the settlement; and the settlers are hereby strictly enjoined to report all such persons as may offend herein. It is proper here also to signify that it is his Excellency's positive injunction to the settlers and others who have firearms that they do not wantonly fire at or take the lives of any of the natives, as such an act would be considered a deliberate murder, and subject the offender to such punishment as (if proved) the law might direct to be inflicted.

It has been intimated to the Governor that there have been frequently seen amongst the natives two white men, who, it is known, have absconded from their duty, and who, it is believed, direct and assist in those acts of hostility by which so many have suffered. It is therefore recommended to all persons in the settlement who have known and have heard of the white men above mentioned, and particularly to the settlers who are so much annoyed by them, that they do use every means in their power to secure them, that they may be so disposed of as to prevent their being hereafter troublesome or dangerous.

The Governor takes this opportunity of strictly forbidding the settlers from giving any encouragement to the natives to lurk about their farms. There can be no doubt but that had they never met with the shelter which some have afforded them they would not at this time have been so very troublesome and dangerous.[4]

The spread of settlement—A 'frontier' problem

No longer was there serious trouble with the natives in Sydney. The following document highlights the fact that the problem was one of the 'frontier':

71 From the wanton manner in which a large body of natives, resident about Parramatta, George's River, and Prospect Hill, have attacked and killed some of Government sheep, and their violent threat of murdering all the white men they meet, which they put into execution by murdering Daniel Conroy, stock-keeper, in a most savage and inhumane manner, and severely wounding Smith, settler; and as it is impossible to foresee to what extent their present hostile menaces may be carried, both with respect to the defenceless settlers and the stock, the Governor has directed that this as well as all other bodies of natives in the above district to be driven back from the settlers' habitations by firing at them. But this order does not extend to the natives in any other district; nor is any native to be

---

[4] Government Order [by Hunter], 22 February 1796, *ibid.*, pp. 688–9.

molested in any part of the harbour, at Sydney, or on the road leading to Parramatta.[5]

> By the end of 1801 the Governor was taking decisive action to prevent crop destruction.

72   A detachment at George's River is to consist of a sergeant, corporal, and six privates until further orders, who are to be posted as follows:—A sergeant and four privates at Major Johnston's, a corporal and two privates at Sergeant-major Jamieson's or Corporal Teutrill's. This detachment is to prevent the natives from firing the wheat, for which purpose a private will patrole occasionally from daylight till nine o'clock at night, and one private to be always ready during the night as a picquet. They are to fire on any native or natives they see, and if they can, pursue them with a chance of overtaking them. Every means is to be used to drive them off, either by shooting them or otherwise, taking care always to leave one private where posted.

A captain is to inspect that post once a week. Similar orders are to be given to the outposts from the Parramatta detachment; an officer from that post will inspect these outposts once a week, or oftener.[6]

> Yet while the Governor's actions were decisive they did not lack humanity.

73   One of the settlers recently fix'd below Portland Head, who was much annoyed by the natives in June last, delivered me a memorial, said to be signed by all the settlers in that district, requesting they might be allowed to shoot the natives frequenting their grounds, who had threatened to fire their wheat when ripe. On further enquiry I found that none of the settlers had authorized this man to put their signatures to the paper, and that his fears of what might be had operated with him more forcibly than any present or future probability of the natives again being inimical to him or his neighbours. As the imposition could not pass by unnoticed, he was sentenced by the magistrates to a month's confinement in the jail; but in consideration of his property being likely to suffer he was released after a few days' confinement. Wishing to be convinced myself what cause there was for these alarms, three of the natives from that part of the river readily came on being sent for. On questioning the cause of their disagreement with the new settlers they very ingenuously answered that they did not like to be driven from the few places that were left on the banks of the river, where alone they could procure food; that they had gone down the river as the white men took possession of the banks;

[5] Government Order [by King], 1 May 1801, *ibid.*, p. 250.
[6] Government Order [by King], 22 November 1801, *ibid.*, pp. 466–7.

if they went across white men's grounds the settlers fired upon them and were angry; that if they could retain some places on the lower part of the river they should be satisfied and would not trouble the white men. The observation and request appear to be so just and so equitable that I assured them no more settlements should be made lower down the river. With that assurance they appeared well satisfied and promised to be quiet, in which state they continue.[7]

> However, when the following year's crop was ripe for harvest, there was further trouble. The natives were not bent upon *taking* the crops but upon destroying them.

74   The implacable spirit of the Branch natives suffers no opportunity of mischief to escape. Since the commencement of the harvest they have made repeated attempts to set fire to the wheat of different settlers, but from some fortunate accident their odious project has failed of success. In one instance they were detected with fire brands in a field of Thos. Duggan, who with assistance repelled them. Every effort has been made by the Magistrate, Gentlemen, and settlers throughout the district, to tranquillize them, but to no effect. Mr. Thomson, chief constable has been repeatedly missioned [*sic*] to enquire into their grievances; and while they offer no subject of complaint, yet they admit the justice of accusation, and promise to desist; but their promises are known to be subject to caprice.[8]

> At times it seemed that a few natives were the ring-leaders, and that if they could be captured the hostilities might cease.

75   The Natives having solicited to return to Sydney and Parramatta no molestation is to be offered to those frequenting the above places provided they behave quietly, otherwise they are to be reported to the Magistrate who will order them to be confined. The Natives about Hawkesbury and Georges River still continue their depredations the General order of the 27th April is to continue in force respecting these places, and it is hoped the apprehension of the native called Musquito might effectually prevent any further mischief in those quarters.[9]

> The native in the following extract would seem to have had a grudge against white men because of his father's death.

---

[7] King to Hobart, 20 December 1804, *ibid.*, v, pp. 512-13.
[8] *Sydney Gazette*, 22 December 1805.
[9] Extract from Orderly Book, 14 October 1804, in W. W. Burton, *Papers relating to Aborigines*, MS. no. A1161, M.L.

76   Some of the distant settlers have had recent occasion to complain of the conduct of the natives, a few among whom have manifested a disposition to mischievous acts. A man of the name of Tunks in company with another was attacked near Parramatta by three blacks, among whom was young *Bundle* and *Tedbury*, the son of *Pemulwoy*, who was shot some years since on account of his murders, and the horrible barbarities he had exercised on many solitary travellers. The son appears to have inherited the ferocity and vices of his father: Upon the above occasion he pointed his spear to the head and breast of Tunks, and repeatedly threatened to plunge the weapon into him, but other persons fortunately appearing in sight, the assailants betook to the woods. Several other such attacks have been made, but as *Tedbury* is stated to have always been of the party, which consisted but of two or three, it may be inferred that a spirit of malevolence is far from general; and under this belief, it may be hoped the settlers will not permit their servants or families to practice unnecessary severities which may irritate, and provoke those who are at present peaceably disposed, to join in the atrocities of a few miscreants, whom their own tribe, if not exasperated by ill treatment, would no doubt as they have frequently done before, betray into our hands, and avowedly assist in apprehending.[10]

The Rev. Samuel Marsden suggested another possible remedy to the problem:

77   ... many of the Aborigines have been murdered the last year, and many of the Europeans by the natives—I had two of my Servants killed by the Natives from the Spirit of Retaliation. These murders would be prevented, if we could get any proper missionaries to live amongst the natives in the interior—honest plain simple men of Principle and Character, men who would be able to learn their Language. As the Europeans are extending into the interior, unless some measures are adopted to prevent Crime, the natives will be extirpated—And this cannot be prevented, but by missionaries. This Country must become very great—its advantages are so many. It would be a great Blessing if we could get a few pious clergymen to itinerate amongst the Inhabitants of the distant Settlements.[11]

The story of the missionary attempts will be told in a later chapter.
  As the settlers moved further away from Sydney, so too did the hostilities, and it became necessary for the colonial authorities to instruct officials in outlying areas to conduct enquiries.

[10] *Sydney Gazette*, 3 September 1809.
[11] Marsden to Pratt, 7 February 1825, Bonwick Transcripts, Box 53, M.L.

78   With reference to your communication of the 18th Instant addressed to the Acting Military Secretary, reporting that Three Native Blacks had been shot by the Mounted Police under the command of Lieut. Low, I am directed by His Excellency the Governor to request that you will in conjunction with Messrs. Close, Webber and Scott assemble and enquire into the particulars of the killing of the Natives alluded to; so that Government may be enabled to determine whether it will be necessary to institute any Proceedings in consequence; but you are not to proceed in the investigation unless Lieut. Low be present.[12]

> The hostilities appeared to increase with the distance, and in some cases involved not only individual settlers but official patrol parties too as the following extract demonstrates:

79   I do myself the honor to forward for your information the accompanying Copy of a Minute of the Proceedings of the Executive Council, together with sundry Documents relating to the subject of a very gross Outrage committed by a Party employed in Patrolling the Neighbourhood of the Settlement of Fort Wellington on the Northern Coast in the Month of December last.

The Case is briefly as follows:—The Commandant, from the very serious annoyance to which the Settlement was subject from the Natives, as pointed out in my Despatch No. 23, and which had been rendered the more alarming from the sickly State of the Troops and the Settlement generally, was induced to offer a Reward for any Native who should be brought in, hoping that, by keeping such Individual at the Settlement, it might have the effect of preventing any further hostility on the part of the Natives at the present moment, and operate hereafter as a means of conciliating them, when, on being released, they should find the Person so detained had been treated with kindness and attention.

This was the motive of the Commandant, but the object was very awkwardly effected by the Party. They appear to have proceeded some distance from the Settlement, when they discovered a large Body of Natives. Being under some apprehension in consequence of the smallness of their own Numbers, they fired on the Natives and wounded four or five at least, amongst whom it afterwards appeared there was a Woman and two Children. The Woman and one of the Children did not survive; the other, a Girl of between 6 and 7 years old, was taken to the Settlement. But it is still more painful to relate that they appear to have despatched an unfortunate Man, who had

---

[12] Colonial Secretary to Captain Allman, Commandant at Newscastle, 28 August 1826, W. W. Burton, *Papers Relating to Aborigines*, MS. no. A1161, M.L.

been wounded by their first fire, from a desire, as they state, of relieving him from his Sufferings, the nature of his Wounds rendering it impossible to remove him. You will perceive, Sir, by the enclosed Documents, that every Step has been taken to prevent a repetition of such a distressing occurrence. But, being desirous of ascertaining whether anything further could be done with reference to the past, I was induced to submit the matter to the Council, and you will see, by the enclosed Minute of Proceedings, that the Council have not been able to suggest the adoption of any further measure.

I informed the Council that I have given Orders that the Men, concerned in this unfortunate Affair, should be sent to Sydney; but it did not appear, much as the Event is to be deplored, that any benefit would result from the further prosecution of the matter. I have however, Sir, deemed it my duty to put you in possession of the case and shall be ready to carry any Orders into effect, which you may be pleased to give me on the subject.

I cannot close my Letter without assuring you that, independant of Captain Smyth's Zeal as an Officer, which entitles him to the warmest approbation of the Government, he is a most conscientious Man, and I am sure entertains as just an abhorrence of the unfortunate Event which occurred under his Command, as any one possibly can.[13]

>Governor Darling's anxiety over this incident was echoed in the official reply from London.

80 I have received your Despatch Marked "Separate" of the 28th of August, 1828, with its enclosures, relating to an attack made on the Natives at the Settlement of Fort Wellington in the month of December, 1827, by a Party from the Garrison at that place, in which three of the Natives are reported to have lost their lives.

I cannot too strongly express my reprobation of the behaviour of all the Persons concerned in this inexcusable transaction.

An unofficered expedition of private Soldiers, and, as it should seem, of Convicts also, undertaken against the Natives upon a promise of a pecuniary reward for the capture of one or more of them, could scarcely tend to any other than the lamentable result which actually followed; and the conduct of Captain Smith, in sending forth or sanctioning it, appears to me to be so very reprehensible, both as relates to the unfortunate people, whose lives have been taken away, and to the honor of the British name, that I have thought it my duty to transmit a Copy of your Despatch with its enclosures, to the Horse Guards for the information of the General Commanding in Chief.

---

[13] Darling to Huskisson, 28 August 1828, *H.R.A.*, I, xiv, pp. 350–1.

With respect to the Individuals who composed the expedition I am of opinion that, after the length of time which has elapsed since the occurrence of these events, and the subsequent recall of His Majesty's Troops from the Settlement, where they occurred it may be proper to acquiesce in the decision of the Council that the matter cannot with advantage be further pursued; but I beg you to make it distinctly and generally understood that, if any outrage should hereafter be perpetrated in any degree resembling that, on which I have now been addressing you, it is the determination of His Majesty's Government to proceed with the utmost severity against every individual who shall be a partaker either as principal or as accessory in its commission.[14]

Eventually it became necessary to make provisions for the protection of Aborigines beyond the boundaries of location. It is interesting to note Gipps' reference to the House of Commons Select Committee Report in making these provisions.

81 In my Despatch No. 67 of the 25th instt., I detailed to your Lordship the measures which I thought it right to adopt, in consequence of a recent collision between a party of the Mounted Police and a Tribe of the Native Blacks, and I have now the honor to acquaint you that I have further deemed it necessary, with the advice of my Executive Council, to issue a Government Notice declaring that, in all cases where any of the Aboriginal Inhabitants of this Territory shall lose their lives in consequence of a quarrel or collision with white men, an Inquest or Inquiry shall be held, precisely similar to that which is held in the located parts of the Territory when a white man comes to a violent or sudden death, and also declaring that the Commissioners of Crown Lands, beyond the Boundaries of Location, shall act as Protectors of Aborigines.

Your Lordship will perceive by the Copy, which I enclose of the proposed Notice and which will appear in the Gazette of Wednesday next, that it is founded partly on your Lordship's Despatch of the 26th July, 1837, No. 353, and partly on the suggestions thrown out in the Report of the Committee of the House of Commons on the treatment of the Aborigines in British Possessions which sat in the last Session of Parliament.

Your Lordship is, I am sure, well aware of the extreme difficulty of devising any measure that shall effectually check the outrages, which, I regret to state, are now of frequent occurrence beyond the boundaries of Location. I may not be very sanguine of the entire success of the one I have resorted to, but, being the only one within my power, I hope it will meet your Lordship's approbation.

[14] Murray to Darling, 3 September 1829, *ibid,.* xv, pp. 153–4.

I have also deemed it necessary to republish a Notice, which appeared in the Government Gazette on the 16th Septt., 1837, on the subject of the forcible retention by white men of women belonging to the Aboriginal Tribes, which there is reason to fear is often the immediate cause of these outrages.[15]

However, in a postscript to this despatch, Gipps stated that further murders by the Aborigines, both to the North and to the South, had rendered it expedient to delay publication of the notices, because of the exasperation felt by the European settlers. The Executive Council expressed concern for the volunteers who composed the Mounted Police, and Gipps conveyed this concern in a 'Separate and Confidential' despatch.

82   Your Lordship must be, I am sure, aware that these matters are calculated to produce a considerable sensation in the Colony, and that therefore much management is required in the treatment of them. In the Executive Council, an apprehension arose of the mischief that might ensue, if any offence were given to the Officers and Men of the Mounted Police, who are (as your Lordship doubtless knows) all Volunteers from Regiments of the Line serving in New South Wales, and at liberty to resign their Police duties and return to their Regiments when they please.[16]

The difficulties were exacerbated by the increasing distance of the scenes of hostility from the seat of government. In one despatch Gipps reported troubles both on the river Gwydir and in the Port Phillip district.

83   I lament to say that we have since heard of some outrages, which have the appearance of being retaliatory on the part of the Blacks. One white man at a distant Cattle station, belonging to a Mr. Fitzgerald, on the river Gwyder [sic], has been most barbarously murdered, and some Cattle belonging to the same person slaughtered in a way that seems also to indicate its having been an act of revenge, rather than one of ordinary rapine, though I am not without hope that they may prove unfounded.[17]

. . .

Atrocities of a still more serious character have also, I regret to say, been reported, since the above Despatch was written, from quite another part of the Country. A party consisting of no less than eighteen men, who were driving a large herd of Cattle and a considerable number of sheep from the County of Murray to Port Phillip, were attacked on the 13th ulto. by a party of 300 Blacks

---

[15] Gipps to Glenelg, 27 April 1838, *ibid.*, xix, pp. 397-8.
[16] *ibid.*, p. 399.
[17] *ibid.*, p. 400.

and eight of them killed. I have as yet no particulars of the occurrence; but I have directed a Civil Stipendiary Magistrate and a party of the Mounted Police to proceed with all possible despatch to the spot.[18]

> As areas like Port Phillip were opened up by white settlers, the government of the colony found itself quite unable to provide adequate protection for either the whites or the Aborigines.

84   On the 18th ulto., a Memorial was transmitted to me by a number of gentlemen interested in the opening of the Country near Port Phillip, of which I enclose a Copy; but, in so doing, as well as in transmitting to your Lordship a copy of my answer to it, it is necessary that I should explain to your Lordship that some of the gentlemen, who signed this Memorial, had previously waited upon me and requested that I would either myself levy war against the Blacks, or sanction the enrolment of a Militia for that purpose and allow them to be supplied with Arms and Munitions of War from Her Majesty's stores; and that it was (as I presume) in consequence of my declining to do either, that their subsequent Memorial was, contrary to usual practice, addressed to the Governor and the Executive Council instead of the Governor alone.

I have the honor to enclose a short abstract of the principal outrages between Blacks and Whites which have been reported in the last three months. Your Lordship will observe that a large proportion of these acts of violence occurred in the neighbourhood of Port Phillip, or on the road between the settled parts of the Colony and that place; the reason of which is that large herds of Cattle and flocks of sheep have been recently driven through these extensive tracts of Country, with a very insufficient number of people to guard them, often not more than in the proportion of one man to several hundred sheep; That, under these circumstances, predatory attacks should have been made on them by the Natives, does not I must say appear to me in the least degree to be wondered at.

Your Lordship must be aware that it is quite out of the power of this Government to give to the proprietors or their Flocks the protection they desire; even if we were restrained by no sense of humanity towards the Blacks, the resources of the Government would be quite insufficient to keep Military parties always in advance of persons who are migrating in search of pasturage, advancing often 50 miles in a single season, and in the case of Port Phillip having stretched to a distance beyond our former limits of between three and four hundred miles in the last three years

---

[18] *ibid.*, postscript dated 2 May 1838.

If Proprietors, for the sake of obtaining better pasturage for their increasing flocks, will venture with them to such a distance from protection, they must be considered to run the same risk as men would do, who were to drive their sheep into a Country infested with wolves, with this difference however that, if they were really wolves, the Government would encourage the shepherds to combine and destroy them, whilst all we can now do is to raise, in the name of Justice and humanity, a voice in favor of our poor savage fellow creatures, too feeble to be heard at such a distance.

Your Lordship will not fail to observe that, of the outrages enumerated in the accompanying list, some took place two or three hundred miles to the North of Sydney, others at more than 500 miles to the South, and some (at Geelong, the Western limit of Port Phillip) at a still greater distance.

In order to keep open the communication between Sydney and Port Phillip, it is my intention, with the concurrence of the officer in command of Her Majesty's Troops, to establish Military Posts on the road; and I forward a sketch on which the places of these proposed posts are marked, they being, as your Lordship will perceive, the places where the road crosses the following streams on the way, vizt., the Murray, the Ovens, the Violet Creek, and the Goulburn.[19]

> Perhaps the best known of all these outbreaks of hostility is the Myall Creek massacre. It represented a significant stage in black-white relations because the Europeans responsible were executed. There are many accounts of this in official despatches, colonial newspapers and so on, but the following extract has been chosen for the summary it gives of the whole episode.

85   In my Despatch of the 21st July last, No. 115, I brought under your Lordship's notice a long list of atrocities, committed both by and on the Aborigines of this Country; and I then stated that I had despatched a party of Mounted Police in search of some white men, who were supposed to have put to death in cold blood not less than twenty two helpless and unoffending Blacks; it is now my painful duty to inform your Lordship that seven of the perpetrators of this atrocious deed, having been convicted on the clearest evidence, suffered yesterday morning the extreme penalty which the law awards for the crime of murder.

The act, for which these men have paid the forfeit of their lives, took place on the evening of Sunday, the 10th June last, at or near a Cattle station, belonging to a person of the name of Henry Dangar,

---

[19] Gipps to Glenelg, 21 July 1838, *ibid.*, pp. 509–10.

distant perhaps 350 miles from Sydney in a direction due North, on the banks of the Myall Creek. This Creek is a branch of the Big River, which is supposed to fall into the sea at Shoal Bay, in about Lat. 29°S.; but your Lordship is aware that this part of the Country is so little known, that it is impossible to fix the spot with any degree of precision. On the banks of the Big River, there are several Cattle stations besides that of Mr. Dangar; and it appeared on the trial that, for some weeks previous to the 10th June, not less than fifty Blacks of all ages and sexes had been living at these different stations (but mostly at Mr. Dangar's) in perfect tranquility, neither molesting the Whites nor being themselves molested by them. In consequence of some old quarrels, however, or possibly from accounts having reached the place of occurrences in other quarters, a determination seems to have been formed by the white men to put the whole of the Blacks to death. On the afternoon of Sunday, the 10th June, a number of them suddenly surrounded the place, where more than thirty of the Blacks were assembled; they tied them all to a rope in the way that Convicts are sometimes tied, in order to be taken from place to place in the Colony, marched them to a convenient spot about a quarter of a mile off, and put them all, with the exception of one woman and four or five children, deliberately to death. The following day, Monday, the 11th June, the same white men scoured the Country on horseback, endeavoring to find ten or twelve of the Blacks, who, having left Dangar's station on the morning of the 10th, had escaped the massacre. These ten or twelve persons have never been seen or heard of since, and it is doubtful to this day whether they were not overtaken and murdered also. The first account of these deeds of blood reached Sydney about the end of the month of June. I despatched, with as little delay as possible, a Stipendiary Magistrate (Mr. Day), on whose activity and discretion I could rely, and a party of Mounted Police, in search of the Murderers; and Mr. Day, after an absence of 53 days, reported to me in person that, having come unexpectedly to the Cattle station of Mr. Dangar, he had succeeded in capturing no less than eleven out of the twelve persons, who were known to have taken part in the massacre. When Mr. Day arrived at the spot, some few scattered human bones only were visible, great pains having been taken to destroy the whole remains of the slaughtered Blacks by fire; but undeniable evidence was procured of more than twenty human heads having been counted on the spot within a few days after the day of the massacre; and the best accounts lead me to suppose that the number of persons murdered of all ages and both sexes was not less than 28.

The eleven persons apprehended by Mr. Day, all arrived in this

Country as Convicts, though, of some of them, the sentences have expired. The twelfth man or the one who has escaped is a free man, a native of the Colony, named John Fleming.

The eleven men were all brought to trial on the 15th Novr. on an information lodged against them by the Attorney General containing nine Counts. The first four Counts charged them in various ways with the murder of an Aboriginal Black named Daddy, the only adult male who could be identified as one of the murdered party; the five other Counts charged them (also in various ways) with the murder of an Aboriginal male Black, name unknown. The Jury on this occasion acquitted the whole of the Prisoners.

The Attorney General immediately applied to have them detained on the further charge of murdering the women and children, none of whom had been comprehended in the first Indictment; and, this being done, seven of these men on the 27th of the same month (November) were again brought before the Supreme Court on the charge of murdering a child. On this occasion, the first five Counts charged them simply with the murder of an Aboriginal Black Child; other Counts described the Aboriginal Child by the name of Charley. The Attorney General laid this information only against seven of the Prisoners, instead of the whole eleven, in order that they might have the opportunity of calling the other four, if they chose to do so, as witnesses in their favor, but which they did not do. On being brought this second time before the Court, the Prisoners, who were defended by three of the ablest Counsel at the Bar, entered on the first five Counts a Demurrer, to the effect that there was not sufficient certainty in the description of the Aboriginal Child, neither the name, nor the sex being mentioned; and against the other Counts of the Indictment, which charged them with the murder of a Boy called Charley, they entered the Plea of "Autre fois acquit", saying that it was the same offence, for which they had been already acquitted. The Presiding Judge (Mr. Justice Burton) overruled their Demurrer, declaring that there was sufficient certainty in the description of the child, though neither the sex nor name was mentioned: and, upon their Plea of "Autre fois acquit", issue being joined by the Attorney General, a Jury was impanelled to try whether the Offence, with which they then stood charged, was or was not the same as that for which they had already been acquitted. This Jury found that it was not the same offence. The seven men were consequently two days afterwards, on the 29th Novr., put on their trial for the murder of the child, and found Guilty on the first five Counts, which described the Child merely as a Black Aboriginal: but were acquitted upon the Counts, which charged them with the murder of a Child named Charley, sufficient proof of the name of the child not being adduced.

The seven men were brought up for judgment on the 5th inst., upon which occasion their Demurrer, as well as their Plea of "Autre fois acquit", was brought under the solemn consideration of the three Judges of the Supreme Court, and sentence of death was not passed upon them, until after the three Judges had unanimously expressed their opinion, against the validity of their Demurrer, and their satisfaction with the verdict of the Jury, which had been empanelled on their plea of "Autre fois acquit".

The Report of the Judge (Mr. Justice Burton), who presided at the trial, was received by myself and the Executive Council on Friday, the 7th instt., when, no mitigating circumstances appearing in favor of any of them, and nothing to shew that any one of them was less guilty than the rest, the Council unanimously advised that the sentence of the law should take effect on them; they were accordingly ordered by me for Execution, and suffered yesterday morning at 9 o'clock.

It will be satisfactory to your Lordship to hear, that the smallest doubt does not exist of the guilt of the men who have been executed, or of their all having been actively engaged in the massacre. The whole eleven would indeed, I have reason to believe, have pleaded guilty at the first trial, if not otherwise advised by their Counsel. After condemnation, none of the seven attempted to deny their crime, though they all stated that they thought it extremely hard that white men should be put to death for killing Blacks. Until after their first trial, they never I believe thought that their lives were even in jeopardy.

Three Petitions were presented to me in their favor, though not very numerously signed, one from Sydney, another from Parramatta, and the third from Windsor, but I did not feel that I could consistently with my public duty pay regard to them.[20]

The Myall Creek massacre did not mark the end of hostilities, and settlers continued to call for protection. However, Governor Gipps observed that no district remained troubled for very long and that the problem could be dealt with by the issuing of special emergency orders, rather than by preventing the movement of white men with their flocks and herds. As he told the Secretary of State:

86 I have the honor to receive Your Lordship's Dispatch No. 66 of the 21st. Feby., 1842, enclosing the Copy of one from the Governor

---

[20] Gipps to Glenelg, 19 December 1838, *ibid.*, pp. 700–4.

of South Australia representing to your Lordship the hostile attitude which had been assumed by the Aborigines in the Neighbourhood of the Murray River about a year ago, and proposing that, in order to guard against a recurrence of acts of outrage and Murder on the line of Communication between Adelaide and Sydney, measures should be taken by the respective Governors of New South Wales and South Australia, to prevent the passage of any parties from one Colony to the other, except under a competent escort to be provided by the Government, but paid for by the parties escorted.

Having been called upon by Your Lordship to express my opinion of the proposal thus made by the Governor of South Australia, I feel bound to state to Your Lordship that, though I entirely concur with the Governor of South Australia in thinking it to be the duty of the Governors of all Her Majesty's Australian Colonies to repress, to the utmost extent of their power, any hostile agressions either by or on the Aborigines, I can see no reason why this should be done more in one part of this Colony than in another, or upon one line of communication rather than upon all. It certainly happened that, in the course of the year 1841, the collisions near the Murray River were more serious than in any other part of either this Colony or South Australia; but their sanguinary nature was I believe rather to be attributed to accidental than permanent causes; and in the history of New South Wales, it has rarely happend for any one District to remain in a troubled state a considerable length of time.

It certainly does not appear to me that the intervention of any superior authority is more necessary in respect to the communication between South Australia and New South Wales, than to those between many of the Districts lying wholly within the Territory of New South Wales, as for instance between the Districts on Rivers falling into the Darling (and ultimately into the Murray), and the Districts of the River Clarence or Moreton Bay, between any of the same Districts and the Country of Corner Inlet, otherwise called Gipps' Land, or even between Sydney and Port Phillip. A reference to my Despatches of the year 1838, . . . will shew that the Port Phillip Road was, for the first two years after it was opened, extremely unsafe, and that some sanguinary collisions took place on it; but Posts, with Mounted Policemen, having been established at intervals along the road, travelling thenceforth became perfectly safe; and, during the last three years, no aggressions of a serious nature have been committed.

Any general regulation, forbidding persons to move Sheep or Cattle from one part of this Colony to another, without being provided with an escort from Government, would be felt, I can have no hesitation in saying, as a grievous hardship; and it would have, I fear, a very bad effect in leading people habitually to disregard the regulations of Government or even the Law itself.

The necessity of moving Sheep or Cattle (on account of Drought or want of Pasturage) is often most urgent; and, even within the last twelve months, very extensive losses have been sustained in the District of Liverpool Plains (North West of Sydney) from the inability of parties to remove their Stock in sufficient time from a Country suffering under drought. Not less than ten thousand head of horned Cattle and thirty thousand sheep are supposed to have perished in this District; yet, so great is the abundance of stock in the Colony, that these losses have only been felt as individual calamities.

I consider it to be quite within my own power to issue an Order, such as Governor Grey did in July, 1841, forbidding communication on any particular line of road except under escort; and, if occasion required it, I should not hesitate to issue such an order, in the same way as I have issued orders that no Squatters shall be Licenced, or allowed to occupy stations, beyond the limits of protection; such special orders can be enforced, whilst general measures prohibiting the removal of Cattle could not.

In the course of the year 1841, it was suggested to me by Governor Grey that I should issue an official Notice, informing the Public of the disasters which had befallen some of the parties, travelling overland from New South Wales to South Australia, and warning them that they should not in future attempt to pass from one Colony to the other without being well armed; such notices however it did not seem to me expedient to issue, first, because full information respecting the conflicts on the Murray had already been given to the Public through the ordinary channels of information, and secondly, because I could not but apprehend that any invitation to parties to arm themselves, proceeding from me, would have been construed into a general permission to take the business of defending, and of avenging themselves too, into their own hands.[21]

> Eight years after Gipps wrote to Lord Glenelg about the events at Myall Creek, he still had to report to London an unsettled state of affairs.

87 I am sorry to have to report to your Lordship that, notwithstanding the exertions of this Government, and the large expenditure now incurred on account of the Aborigines, the acts of violence, committed by or on them, continue in some parts of the Colony to increase, and especially in the neighbourhood of Portland Bay, and the Country to the North of it, forming the Western and most remote part of the District of Port Phillip.[22]

---

[21] Gipps to Stanley, 11 August 1842, *ibid.*, xxii, pp. 197–9.
[22] Gipps to Stanley, 2 December 1846, *ibid.*, p. 386.

Suggested Remedies

Occasionally a white person would question the reason for native attacks. One white woman, the wife of a settler, sought not only the cause but also looked for a remedy.

88 The Aborigines both at Hunter River, and in the New Country (Argyle) are still very hostile—several murders have been of late committed by them in the former District, and altho the Mounted Police have been actively engaged in pursuit of them, and have in these affrays shot two or three, yet they seem so far from being intimidated that they become daily more and more daring—things indeed now have gone so far that something decisive must be done to stop the progress of this evil, or the Stockmen and Shepherds will not be readily persuaded to remain at the distant settlements, while exposed to the animosity of a set of untutored Savages.—As these Natives have never before been known to proceed to such extremities, there is reason I think some *motive* must exist for their present warfare, which if possible should be ascertained, and if six or eight of them could be brought in as Prisoners, it is likely we should become acquainted with the cause of their animosity, and probably find it easy of remedy: perhaps our people have been the first aggressors, or probably a want of food may drive them to desperate measures. . . .[23]

The responsibility for Aboriginal hostilities was placed by one newspaper at the door of the whites: whites goaded the Aborigines while other whites aided them.

89 In consequence of the depredations and murders committed by the black natives, headed we understand by bushrangers, at Williams' River, and in the neighbourhood of Mr. McQueen's estate of Segenhoe, Major Croker and four subalterns with upwards of fifty rank and file of the 17th Regt., were dispatched to Hunter's River, on Monday evening last, by order of His Excellency the Governor, to protect the district, and to capture or otherwise punish the offenders. We have been informed that the supposed origin of the aggressions of the blacks is the indiscriminate desire of vengeance excited by the injuries they are constantly experiencing at the hands chiefly of ticket-of-leave and free men, who are allowed to go at large beyond the stations of settlers in the distant parts of the territory. There ought surely to be a Vagrant Act passed to enable the Executive to sieze and punish all persons at large in this way. It is not less necessary for the protection of the black

---

[23] Christiana Brooks, Diary, entry 11 September 1826, MS. no. 1559, National Library of Australia.

natives than for that of the whites. At the same time we cannot help remarking, how inefficient a description of force officers and soldiers of the hire must necessarily be for such a service as Major Croker and the other officers and soldiers of the 17th Regt. are now detached upon. However able the officers and brave the men, what can either officers or men do, comparatively speaking, in a country of which they must necessarily be entirely ignorant, and in which they must be in danger of losing themselves at every step. The experience necessary for such service can only be acquired by a residence of years in the country.[24]

> But generally speaking the reaction of the whites was one of righteous indignation and impatience with any measures to understand and make excuses for the Aborigines.

90   In glancing over the columns of your contemporaries of last week (says a writer in a Van Diemen's Land paper) I observe a remark to the following effect:—"We hope the atrocities of the Aborigines will now cease, as Black Tom is dead". By this and other such pusillanimous writers, is the atrocious acts of these savages varnished over, and the due punishment of them retarded. 'Tis a great pity this person, instead of being seated in his comfortable parlour, taking his wine and writing fine ridiculous speeches about the sudden and immediate reformation of the savage hearts of those sable villains, by the death of one of their party, was placed alone at some distant stock-hut, where those whose cause he advocates, could repay his pernicious kindness.—I augur he would find Black Tom's spirit revived in the heart of every savage native in the island. For the last four years the murders that have been committed by those sable tribes, at a moderate computation, amount at least to seventy or eighty persons. If all those victims were brought out and despatched with spears and waddies, at once, in front of Government-house in Macquarie Street, it would not alter the fact one jot—such an horrid scene would fire every bosom with a just revenge, but those unfortunate victims, dying one by one, excite little or no attention. Our Rulers must do something to prevent these murders, or they forfeit all claims to the feelings of humanity for ever. The wandering shades of so many murdered victims loudly call for revenge and justice.

   I have no doubt, Mr. Editor, your Correspondent has given you a faithful account as delivered to him by the party who followed the Natives who murdered Mr. Davidson's men at Elizabeth River; but the truth of their statement, of having killed twenty, is justly

---

[24] *Colonist*, 11 June 1835.

suspected, when I assure you, not a dead body, or the least marks of blood, could be found on the following day, after a most diligent search for several hours, where the action was reported to have taken place.—I believe not a single Native was killed.[25]

A popular concept was the inevitability of the destruction of the Aboriginal race in the face of white advancement. Referring to an incident concerning Major Mitchell, a correspondent to the *Sydney Herald* wrote:

91   ... it is in the order of nature that, as civilization advances, savage nations *must* be exterminated ... the Major was not to suffer his party to be sacrificed out of deference to the opinions of associated political and humbugging maniacs and hypocrites who write and prate of matters of which they know nothing whatever.[26]

Reporting native attacks on settlers at Patrick's Plains the *Australian* commented:

92   It does not appear from the statement which has been made to us, what is the reason of a revival of hostilities by the Natives in the above quarter. We have reason, however, to suspect that they did not originate in the misconduct of Overseers or Stockmen, but solely in the bad disposition of the Blacks.—Should this suspicion prove true, we should recommend such decisive measures to be adopted, as will convince these sable depredators, that they cannot attack the peaceable Settlers with impunity—But whatever may be done in the way of reprisal or punishment; it would be advisable to station in this disturbed neighbourhood, a few of the Mounted Police.[27]

The same newspaper claimed that kindness was useless where the Aborigines were concerned. The following article seems to attribute motives to the Aborigines more characteristic of Europeans. The suggested remedy was totally out of keeping with official policy.

93   The Aboriginal Natives in the neighbourhood of Hunter's River are continuing their annoyances, and exhibiting the most malicious designs against the settlers, their stockmen and overseers. They are represented to be past the influence of remonstrance, and seem to have been excited by a very extraordinary cause to make their incursions. It is related of them that they have acquired the notion that blankets, &c. have only been given to them by the Governor to ensure their good will and render them inoffensive, and that they have expressed their determination not to be bribed

[25] *Australian*, 15 June 1827.
[26] *Sydney Herald*, 26 December 1836.
[27] *Australian*, 17 June 1826.

to preserve peace with the white people. If this be true, the remedy against them has been much mistaken, and acts of kindness entirely thrown away upon a race of beings who give very strong proofs that they can only be marshalled into obedience at the point of the bayonet. It is vain to temporize with savages, who have only cunning enough to comprehend that their enemies—enemies only in their own imagination—desire to conciliate them, and who have no capacity to understand that it will promote their own welfare to live on friendly terms with their co-occupants of the territory. With such foes—if foes they can be called—with such tribes, there is but one course to be adopted. If they are insensible to that mode of treatment, which humanity and not fear—as they may imagine—dictates, they must be taught to feel that force of which they seem ignorant. We are by no means friendly to severities; but settlers and their servants, when they conduct themselves peaceably, must be protected, though it be by the sacrifice of the lives of Aborigines. To strike these with terror, by the discriminating application of fire-arms, will ultimately prove a saving of human life, and leave the people in the quiet enjoyment of their farms.[28]

> When the Governor refused to send an armed force into the interior to suppress native outrages, on the grounds that he could not sanction any proceedings unauthorized by the law, the *Colonist* published a letter signed by 'Anti-Humbug'.

94 I am willing to allow His Excellency his meed of praise for his unwillingness to proceed to extremities with these rapacious savages, but his humanity should keep even pace with justice, for it is only justice that the settlers should receive a share of the protection afforded by that government which awards it to the Aboriginal natives themselves. And as to the legality of the proceeding, I would ask His Excellency whether the British law does not recognise the right of a man to use violence in defence of his family, his person, or his property, in case other and milder methods should be found unavailing. Why then should those persons whose necessities oblige them to proceed far into the wilderness be obliged to put up with the injuries they daily receive from these native robbers, who are emboldened by the impurity [*sic*] with which their atrocities have hitherto been perpetrated? If, by one decisive step, the Aborigines are shown their own weakness, and convinced that it is useless for them to contend with Europeans, they will submit and cease their outrages, and much blood shed may be spared. I should regret to see any unnecessary violence made use of towards them; but unless prompt measures are adopted, these dusky "lords

---

[28] *ibid.*, 28 June 1826.

of the soil" will fairly drive the pale faces from their territories—and the result will be, the enacting of the "black war" of Van Dieman's [sic] Land on a much larger scale. Hoping that ere long, means will be taken to secure the lives and properties of our fellow subjects in the bush; and that mistaken humanity (which is but another name for cruelty) may give way to justice.[29]

[29] *Colonist*, 20 June 1838.

4
The Aborigines' White Problem

The Benefits and Brutalities of White contact

Governor Macquarie had his Native Establishment placed on a 'distant fertile tract' because the increase of European population had driven the natives away from Sydney. (Doc. 58) This distant area was, in fact, some ten miles west of Parramatta, at Black Town, now an outer suburb of Sydney. The Rev. Robert Cartwright, the author of the plan to settle the Aborigines in a village community, feared not only disturbance by vagrants, but also retardation of Aboriginal advancement by frequent contact with whites.

95 When informed of the intention of the Committee to apprentice the Boys to the most useful mechanical trade, and to put the Girls out to Service, from my long experience of men and things, and more particularly during the last ten years, in which I have resided in this Colony, I confess my Spirit was damp't at the mention of such a measure, perceiving no cause to believe it would tend to the Moral and spiritual improvement of these savage Youths. The only security for their gradual and real improvement, and which is the opinion of many with whom I have conversed on the Subject, is to keep them as much and as long separate as possible from the bad example of those around them; And if the British Government would locate a quantity of Land, and afford other indulgences to this Institution, similar to what it has done for our Orphan Institution, and for the comfort of those who have been sent here for their crimes, but in some remote and fertile part of the Colony, and there form a Settlement and a Seminary for these black Natives on a good solid plan for their improvement in the knowledge of our useful Arts, as well as in the knowledge and practise of our most holy religion, I think no person will venture to deny that such a plan, so consistent both with reason and revelation, is not likely to ensure the most certain, ample, and speedy success. Here, both boys and Girls should be kept usefully employed 'till they become Men and Women, and are inclined to be, or are capable of becoming Settlers; and then if they should marry, I would recommend a Small portion of this land, with Stock and other necessaries, to be given to them according to their merit. Such an Institution, when once properly established, if managed right, would, I conceive, be carried on with comparatively little expense, since we might reasonably expect it would in great measure supply its own wants, and in time become a most useful and important member of our community.[1]

> This fear of the detrimental effects of white contact was not always apparent. As was noted, in Chapter 2, some of the very earliest attempts to 'civilize' the natives were made by adopting Aboriginal children into white families. In 1810, a correspondent signing himself 'A Friend to Civilization' wrote a long letter which extended over four editions of the *Sydney Gazette*. The essence of the letter was that, as the adults were beyond redemption, the children should be sought out and introduced to civilization. He summarized his argument:

96 I have urged the necessity of adopting as many of the native children as we can procure, and making them members of our own families; and although, perhaps, few parents, whatever be their colour, might upon a short correspondence be inclined to part with their young, yet a few in the first instance kindly treated and properly attended to might, and doubtless would, in the course of time beget a more general confidence; and then, insted of parting with them with reluctance, they would be happy to consent to the alteration of their condition. Upon the other hand, few European families would readily undertake the nurture of a little alien, against whose complexion our prejudices in a manner are at war: but this second obstacle in time may also be surmounted, if humanity be allowed to plead in their behalf. They must be kindly treated, clothed, lodged, and supported in a comfortable manner;—as they learn our language they must be exercised in their own, which our children should acquire;—they must be educated, and instructed in light professions, or in any to which their inclinations lead;—they must be taught to honour their parents, to esteem their relatives, and by counsel and example to contribute as much as possible to the general work of civilization.[2]

> Yet one reader saw inherent dangers in this kind of approach, dangers arising from the poor attention given to their own children by many white parents.

[1] Cartwright to Macquarie, 6 December 1819, *H.R.A.*, I, x, p. 265.
[2] *Sydney Gazette*, 11 August 1810.

97   The children of the Natives ought not to be allowed a mixed intercourse with our own, but kept as a separate flock reserved for a particular purpose; because that if they be as carelessly attended to in their moral progress as our own children too commonly are, they will in all probability exchange ignorance for vice, one to be pitied, the other to be detested. . . . But it is my idea, that the infant natives should have an impartial trial, or else they had better have none at all; for it certainly would be better that they should continue in an uncivilized state, than be polished merely to become corrupt.[3]

Some natives certainly did become corrupt, even though they were not adopted by European families. The following extract from a letter by the missionary William Walker is typical of the observations made by those deeply concerned for the welfare of the Aborigines.

98   Another objection to this settlement [Black Town] is its nearness to Sydney. The natives, instead of cultivating the ground, come to spend the day in idleness, beggary, and drunkenness. Scarcely a Sabbath day dawns that does not witness the majority of the tribe, beastly drunk. Government orders have been issued, the purport of which is, that the person who gives, or allows to be given, any liquor to the blacks, so as to intoxicate them shall fall under the Governor's highest displeasure. The Rev. William Cowper has frequently written to the public; by means of the Gazette; and his papers have discharged his soul. But neither "orders", nor "appeals" and "Monitors", has been able to effect that which is so desirable: viz. That Englishmen would not make the Aborigines worse than they are.

The blacks are much addicted to swearing. This they learn from Englishmen. Judge then, dear Father, what my feelings must be, to behold nakedness, drunkenness, and to hear the most horrid imprecations, in the midst of the flock.[4]

This adoption of the white man's vices led missionaries and civilizers to seek to influence Aborigines in places far removed from European settlements. John Harper, a young Wesleyan missionary, was sent to Wellington Valley to work among Aborigines 'to whom the infection of European wickedness has not extended'.[5] He did not remain there long, and when a more permanent mission was established there the missionaries' main problems stemmed from the white settlers who had by then reached that district. (See chapter 6.)

One attempt to overcome the problem of contact with white men was to allocate grants of land to missionary societies.

---

[3] *ibid.*, 8 September 1810.
[4] Walker to Watson, 8 November 1821, Bonwick Transcripts, Box 52, M.L.
[5] *Sydney Gazette*, 29 September 1825.

99   The Aborigines are in a state of great degradation, and have been much injured by their intercourse with Europeans: the thinking and conscientious people of the Colony feel that these first possessors of the soil have the very strongest claim on those who have planted themselves on their shores, and will liberally support such efforts as shall be made to bring them into possession of the enjoyments of civilized life and the higher blessings of Christianity. Sir Thomas Brisbane, in the grants of land to be occupied for the express benefit of these people, has laid, it may be hoped, a sure foundation for the permanent and successful exertions of the different societies.[6]

Decay of the race predicted

It seemed to many white observers that the Aborigines would not long withstand the European invasion. While not considering white depredations to be deliberate, Archdeacon Broughton believed they were fatal to the Aborigines. He was questioned by the House of Commons Select Committee on Aborigines:

100   Was the consequence of our settlement to drive them away from possessions which they had previously occupied?—Certainly it was, excepting that they had full liberty to remain if they chose; but the effect of our settlement in the country is to drive the kangaroo away, which is their principal means of subsistence. That is an animal that disappears immediately wherever there is a settled habitation of men. They [the Aborigines] still haunt and continue in their natural places, portions belonging to other tribes; they certainly return to it, and seem to linger about it; but they have no settled place, properly so called; it is all occupied by Europeans.

Then they have gradually retired before the progress of our civilization?—I am afraid they do not so much retire as decay; they seem to me to wear out, from some cause; wherever Europeans meet with them, they appear to wear out, and gradually to decay; they diminish in numbers.

Can you explain more specifically that cause?—The tribe is gradually reduced from its original number to a much smaller number; it is a continual process of decay I should think, and it leads me to apprehend, that within a very limited period, those who are very much in contact with Europeans will be utterly extinct; I will not say exterminated, but they will be extinct.

Is this occasioned by the Europeans interfering with their usual habits, and depriving them of their means of hunting, and so on, or by direct ill treatment?—Less by ill treatment than by depriving

[6] *C.M.S. Missionary Register*, 1827, pp. 120–21.

them of the means of subsistence; because, wherever the country is cultivated, the kangaroo disappears; and another very serious cause is the introduction of intoxicating liquors, which destroy great numbers of them.

Then, in fact, our contact with the natives has been productive of great evil to them?—Without any absolute ill usage of them, it certainly does appear to affect them very injuriously; without outrage practised against them. I do not attribute it to actual destruction of them by force, but there is something in our manner and state of society which they appear to decay before.

Is that answer applicable to their temporal condition or their moral and religious character, or both?—They appear actually to vanish from the face of the earth; they diminish in number; and, as I mentioned just now, I think it must in a few years occasion them to be utterly extinct, wherever Europeans are thickly settled.[7]

> The cruelty with which they had been treated served to hasten their inevitable extermination, according to James Dredge, a one-time Assistant-Protector of Aborigines. He reported that the number of the Bangerangs had dropped from two hundred to eighty in ten years.

101   They have been treated *cruelly*; their moral and spiritual maladies urgently required the balm of sovereign mercy, but in place thereof they have been drenched with the wormwood and the gall wrung out from the dregs of society too pestilential to be retained in uncontrolled contact with moral and virtuous society. Thus, from the outset, a shade of deeper night was thrown upon their darkness—the iron which had entered their soul received a more deadly thrust; and they commenced their acquaintance with the white man's character and conduct under circumstances which served rather to confirm them in their own previous debased habits, and to exert upon the process of their degredation a force which is rapidly hurrying them on through scenes of indescribable suffering and wretchedness, towards utter extermination.[8]

> Edward Curr, in recalling the 1840s, believed that the natives' abandonment of healthy pursuits for begging after white man's commodities, had much to do with the decrease in their numbers.

102   ... There was, however, no doubt, a tendency to disease consequent on the partial abandonment of their traditional ways of life for others less healthy, for, after my settlement in their country,

---

[7] Evidence before the Select Committee on Aborigines (British Settlements), 1835, *B.P.P.*, Vol. VII, p. 17.
[8] James Dredge, *Brief Notices of the Aborigines of New South Wales* . . ., Geelong, 1845, pp. 14–15.

the Bangerangs gave up in great measure their wholesome and exhilarating practices of hunting and fishing, and took to hanging about our huts in a miserable objectless frame of mind and underfed condition, begging and doing trifling services of any sort. . . . Besides these causes of decrease it must also be stated that infanticide increased, whilst a certain listlessness and want of interest in life which sprung up under the pressure of our occupation had perhaps something to do with the reduction of the tribe.[9]

> Not only did white man deprive the Aborigine of his hunting grounds and food supplies, but he also drove him into the land of hostile tribes where he could not hope to exist for long.

103 The Christian community of England ought to respond to the feeling which I am happy to say exists in some breasts here, and make the nation ring with loud reiterated peals, against a base system of Colonization which deprives so large a portion of our fellow creatures of their land and food—makes them mendicants and marauders—exposes them to the abuses, and I am sorry to add murders of the unfeeling, the aggrieved settlers—as well as driving them back tribe upon hostile tribe and thus bringing them into barbarous exterminating collision with each other.[10]

> Giving evidence to the 1849 Select Committee on the Aborigines and Protectorate, the Superintendent of Port Phillip said:

104 In the case of the Australian Aborigines, it is difficult to conceive that any other results than a gradual extinction of race could be the ultimate consequence of their peculiar habits and mode of life. But, the fact, that the presence and example of civilization, and introduction of the habits, and vices—more than all, of the European, has connected what may have been a gradual decline, into a rapid fall, cannot be doubted.[11]

> The three following documents depict a common attitude towards the Aborigines. The Rev. W. Yate, questioned while giving evidence to the Select Committee on Aborigines, gave an answer that was to be heard frequently.

105 Must it be acknowledged that the aborigines of Sydney have been treated as degraded creatures, unsusceptible of improvement, and hopelessly brutalized?—Yes, I think so. I have heard again and again people say that they were nothing better than dogs, and that

---
[9] Edward M. Curr, p. 107.
[10] Extract of a letter from the Rev. Joseph Orton, Port Phillip, 5 January 1841, Bonwick Transcripts, Box 54, M.L.
[11] *N.S.W.L.C.V.P.*, 1849, p. 7.

it was no more harm to shoot them than it would be to shoot a dog when he barked at you.[12]

> Edward Curr told a story from his own experiences in the 1840s that illustrated this point. Curr came upon a native wounded in the arm by a hut-keeper's gun. The Aborigine had laid down his own weapons before entering the hut, but had not understood the white man's orders to leave. Curr questioned the hut-keeper—a former convict and soldier.

106   ... As I told him what I thought of his cowardly and barbarous act, he replied, looking at me with the most self-satisfied air, his hands in his breeches pockets, "As many of them as comes here when I'm alone I'll shoot".

"And if it comes to my ears", said I, "that you do anything of the sort, I shall certainly report the fact to the Government."

At this speech "Jack the Soldier", as he was called, seemed quite taken aback! At first he appeared to doubt his ears, ... Even after, I dare say, he looked on me as a sort of dangerous lunatic for troubling myself about the lives of a few Blacks, which he evidently thought he had a perfect right to dispose of as he chose, so long as he did not get into trouble.[13]

> In evidence before the 1845 Select Committee on the condition of the Aborigines, Bishop Polding listed causes of the decrease in the native population. His first point was that the decline was caused by:

107   The aggressive mode of taking possession of their country, which necessarily involves a vast loss of life to the native population. This is done under the influence of principles and ideas which parties, to soothe remorse of conscience, under the influence of selfish motives, are willing to adopt. I have myself heard a man, educated, and a large proprietor of sheep and cattle, maintain, that there was no more harm in shooting a native, than in shooting a wild dog. I have heard it maintained by others, that it was in the course of Providence, that the blacks should disappear before the white, and the sooner the process was carried out the better, for all parties. I fear such opinions prevail to a great extent. Very recently in the presence of two clergymen, a man of education narrated, as a good thing, that he had been one of a party who had pursued the blacks, in consequence of cattle having been rushed by them, and that he was sure they shot upwards of a hundred.—When expostulated with, he maintained that there was nothing wrong in

---

[12] Select Committee on Aborigines (British Settlements) 1835, *B.P.P.*, Vol. VII, p. 202.
[13] Edward M. Curr, *op. cit.*, pp. 53–4.

it, that it was preposterous to suppose they had souls. In this opinion he was joined by another educated person present.[14]

Alcohol and Prostitution

The European vices that played the greatest havoc in the lives of Australian Aborigines were alcohol and prostitution. It is interesting to note the attitude (frequently expressed) that the native women adopted these vices more readily than the men. A man who had lived in Australia wrote:

108 We have been at some pains, during nearly twenty years' residence in that southern world, and being ourselves always warmly interested in the temperance question, to trace the connection between drink and mission failure. If one under missionary teaching be brought into contact with drink, a little will excite him, shame will seize him, he dare not meet the eye of his moral guardian, and he rather quits the field of missionary labour, and retires to his native barbarism. It would be absurd for that minister to tell the poor savage that he should learn to like his glass, with the same ease and equanimity as he himself could do. It will take ages for them to arrive at our standard of respectable tippling; and in the trial, their race dies out. We have conversed with men, who have conducted these missions,—Church of England, Wesleyan, German. Their uniform argument is, that nothing could be done for the blacks, while at large among the whites. That evil springs from the drink in which they indulge, and which is moral death to the blacks. As we have shown before, though the man may resist its influence awhile, the woman is almost directly vanquished. Hence, strange to say, and only to be accounted for on this ground, the male visitants of Mission Stations were far more numerous than those of the other sex. The signal want of success with the females—those who are earliest, easiest, and most strongly affected by European vices—renders the arm of the missionary powerless to reach the men of the tribes.[15]

Nevertheless some Aboriginal men benefited from the activities of their women.

109 Personal prostitution among those associating with the whites is carried on to a great extent, the husbands disposing of the favours of their wives to the convict-servants for a slice of bread or a pipe of tobacco. The children produced by this intercourse are generally sacrificed, . . . the husband usually enforcing the death.[16]

[14] *N.S.W.L.C.V.P.*, 1845, p. 10.
[15] *The Scottish Review*, Glasgow, 1860, p. 390.
[16] Peter Cunningham, *Two Years in New South Wales*, p. 186.

Some of the horror of the white man's treatment of Aborigines is revealed in this letter from the Rev. William Watson, a missionary at Wellington Valley.

110 The White men at the different stations . . . have laboured hard to prevent the Blacks and their children from coming to me. There is a great spirit of Revenge manifested against me because I have opposed the abominable practice of living in adultery and fornication with Black women and Black girls. Your soul would be horrified in the extreme if you were acquainted with only a fraction of the circumstances that have come to my knowledge. A short time ago we had a little girl about 8 or 9 years of age, she went away with her Father. I am told a Stockman whom I know well is living with her as his wife and that this monster of Iniquity has sometimes 3 or 4 such children living with him at the same time, in this manner. 3 weeks ago a girl came here and remains (perhaps she is 10 or 11 years of age) with us. She had the Disease, and told me it was given her by a Stockman about 3 miles from me.[17]

Watson was constantly on the watch to prevent the women from being lured away by white men.

111 I was near the camp of the Natives late tonight and detected two men attempting to persuade some of the females to accompany them to their homes. I was the means for that time however of frustrating their wicked purposes, such are our trials.[18]

The Rev. Dandeson Coates, Secretary of the Church Missionary Society, included some observations on the Aboriginal females of Wellington Valley in a letter to Lord Glenelg.

112 There is perhaps amongst no Aboriginal females a more general willingness to be instructed than is found amongst these; and it is a most affecting circumstance that, on account of the inefficiency of the means forthcoming for the support of the Mission, a more eligible system than the present one could not hitherto be adopted for bringing them into a closer and a more intimate connexion with the female members of the Mission, by whose constant care and instruction, under the Divine Blessing, there is no doubt they would become faithful wives, tender mothers, and useful members of society. It is however a lamentable fact that those, who are under instruction but sleep at the camp, can scarcely go a short distance to fish, etca., without being drawn into evil by Europeans, who sometimes prevail upon them to accompany them

---

[17] Extract from letter, 4 February 1833, Church Missionary Society microfilmed archives relating to the Australian and New Zealand Mission 1808-84.
[18] Watson to Hill, 15 September 1835, *ibid*.

to their huts, and remain with them for the night. The following morning the females have been so ashamed as on that account to absent themselves from the means and place of instruction.[19]

According to Watson, this problem of Europeans seducing the Aborigines was not confined to the 'lower orders'.

113 I am sure your heart would sicken, had you any idea of the moral wretchedness with which we are surrounded. Amongst the hundreds of Europeans who live in this neighbourhood whether Masters, overseers, or servants, scarcely an individual is to be found who has any fear of God before his eyes; and a very large majority of them, live in the violation of every moral principle. On some establishments, where there are from 30 to 40 servants, scarcely a hut can be found, where there is not a native female living in adulterous connexion with the European inmates.[20]

In response to a suggestion by Captain Grey, who had commanded an expedition into the interior of Western Australia, that Aborigines could be easily 'civilized' by attaching them to settlers, the Wesleyan missionary Benjamin Hurst wrote to La Trobe to disagree with the idea.

114 But if the Natives should be attached to the Stations of Settlers, it is difficult to conceive what opportunities they would have of receiving scriptural instruction. Even supposing a Missionary were to be appointed to travel from Station to Station, yet, however zealously and faithfully he might discharge the duties of his object, but little good could be expected to result from his labours. The Native would constantly have before him the bad example of Europeans, and this would go very far towards counteracting any beneficial effects that might result from the labours of the Missionary. But this is not all, for such is the morally degraded condition of the white population, that numbers would be found ready on all occasions to instil evil principles into the mind of the heathen, and thereby sink them lower in depravity and wretchedness than he is at present found. This I think is evident from the fact that although there is a severe legislative enactment against giving intoxicating liquor to the Natives yet the practice is still continued, but continued in such a way that the offending party cannot be convicted at least unless the testimony of the Natives be received.

In connexion with this subject ought also to be mentioned the awful and alarming extent to which the females are prostituted. I am persuaded that no one but he who has occasion to mix frequently with the Natives can form a correct opinion upon this subject. I

---

[19] Coates to Glenelg, 31 October 1838, *H.R.A.*, I, xix, p. 662.
[20] Watson to Jowitt, 17 January 1837, C.M.S. microfilmed archives.

would not rashly come to conclusions upon a point in which my countrymen are so deeply and so disgracefully concerned, but I have for my guidance in forming an opinion, first, the statements of the Natives as to who the persons are that are accustomed to descend to this abominable practice, secondly, the almost universal prevalence among them of a loathsome disease which brings many of them to an untimely death, thirdly, the testimony of medical men as to the extent to which the same disease prevails among Europeans. From these sources of information I am driven to the conclusion that an attempt to civilize this people by attaching them to the Stations of the Settlers would not only fail, but would be inflicting one of the greatest possible evils upon a people who are already sinking under the hand of oppression. We have heretofore abstained from alluding to the share of guilt which attached to individuals who would deem it an insult to be classed with shepherds and hut keepers. But now that the welfare of the people for whose benefit we left our native land is so deeply involved in the question, I think it is time to speak out. I have therefore no hesitancy in informing Your Honour that there is every reason (excepting only absolute proof) to believe that the prostitution of the Native women is not confined to the lower order of Europeans. From these circumstances it appears to me that should Captain Grey's plan be adopted, one of the most effectual measures would be taken to annihilate the wandering tribes of Australia, especially when I call to mind the fact that the half caste children are destroyed almost as soon as they are born.[21]

Undermining by the 'lower orders'

> One of the greatest and most constant complaints made by missionaries and others zealous in the attempt to 'civilize' the Aborigines, was the deliberate attempts made by the 'lower orders' to undermine their philanthropic efforts. William Porter, the Agricultural Assistant at Wellington Valley, complained bitterly of this.

115 My great complaint is the wicked servants we have upon our Establishment. The very fact that they have all been convicts is enough. I do not feel justified in trusting them with anything. The generality of them are indolent, and sometimes very insolent. It is often necessary to send some of our Natives with them in different employments, they not infrequently quarrel with them, if this is not the case, they teach them all lewd songs, and wicked and filthy expressions and I would beg leave to ask the Society if these are proper persons to be kept on a Christian Mission? Any Christian

---

[21] Hurst to La Trobe, 22 July 1841, Bonwick Transcripts, Box 54, M.L.

who thinks upon the subject, will at once say, if he speaks candidly, that it is preposterous. We aim at setting up the Kingdom of Christ in the hearts of these poor brethren—our own servants do all they can, to pull it down again. . . . our greatest object either is, or ought to be, to convert these poor heathen to the faith of Jesus Christ, and experience tells us that there is no civilization without evangelization. . . . Every individual employed on a Christian Mission ought to be a Christian for I am sure every other person will not have the patience that is necessary to be exercised towards these Natives.[22]

James Günther reported the insubordination of a servant who deliberately undermined his wife's disciplinary control of an Aboriginal girl.

116 I also was annoyed this evening about the woman just sent up from Sydney. Mrs. G. had given something to one of the Native Girls to be cleaned and when the girl showed her work to Mrs. G. she desired her to do it a little better, the Girl endeavoured to do so and then the woman who was just in the hut with the children told the girl, "If that will not do let Mrs. G. do it herself", and that is the woman who is expected to assist us in directing the girls in their work! Not to speak of the little qualifications she has for a servant.[23]

There were some cases where whites frightened the natives away from the missions by lies.

117 Some of the Blacks who were staying here, have left us, on account of the lying report of one of the Settlers in our neighbourhood, who told them that there were soldiers coming from Bathurst, who would take away all the Blacks that were near Wellington. It appears to be the anxious desire of our white neighbours, to prevent the Blacks from staying with me, and to hinder our work in various ways.[24]

William Watson claimed that a mission station could never be approved of by inhabitants of a penal colony.

118 No doubt it has reached you, that our Mission is *unpopular* in the Colony. Look at the State of Society here, and let me ask, can the cause of the Redeemer be popular with the devoted servants of the prince of darkness? When the generality of the people labour to encourage the Aborigines in all kinds of vice, no wonder, if the

---

[22] Porter to Cowper, 31 October 1838, C.M.S. microfilmed archives.
[23] James Günther, 15 May 1838, Journal 1836–65, M.L. MSS. B504.
[24] J. S. C. Handt, Journal, 29 January 1835, C.M.S. microfilmed archives.

Aborigines prefer such associations, to living with us under spiritual instruction. We need your Xn sympathies—we need your prayers. Our trials, mental trials are beyond your conception.[25]

> Whites occasionally used their own national rivalries to poison Aboriginal attitudes to missions, as this story shows. Mrs Watson and Mrs Gunther had gone to some trouble to turn a consignment of blankets into dresses for the women and cloaks for the men 'for the sake of decency'. The Aborigines were delighted, yet a few days later some of the men had unpicked the stitching to turn the cloaks back into blankets:

119   ... and, the reason they assign for so doing, is, that these were 'Irish cloaks'. It is not unlikely that some of the wicked Europeans, surrounding us, have put this notion in their heads, perhaps to annoy us. It is curious, however, our Natives commonly attach some idea of inferiority to what is Irish and Ireland, as we have observed in other instances.[26]

> The results of Aboriginal association with lower class whites became readily observable. As Governor Darling told the Secretary of State:

120   ... notwithstanding their Association with the English, it seems impossible for them to abandon their Vagrant habits, or to enter into any pursuit with an appearance of Industry. In short, their habits are those of Mankind in a Savage State; and it is impossible to say, however anxious we may be, that their advancement to Civilization is obvious or satisfactory. The appearance of the Natives about Sydney is extremely disgusting; those, who reside at a distance, are a much finer race, which may in some degree be accounted for by their not having such frequent access to the use of Spirits, in which the former indulge to a Most injurious and disgusting excess.[27]

> Others noticed the difference between the native 'fringe-dwellers' and those who lived in the interior. The Rev. W. Yate commented on this in his evidence before the Select Committee on Aborigines.

121   The Committee understand that you resided some time at Sydney?—I have paid several visits to Sydney, and one of my visits extended to a period of six months.
   Did you devote much attention to the condition of the aborigines of that colony?—I was much struck with the difference between those who are living in the interior and those who are in the neighbourhood of the large towns, such as Sydney and Parramatta.

---

[25] Watson to Jowitt, 17 January 1837, *ibid*.
[26] James Günther, Journal, 30 December 1837, *ibid*.
[27] Darling to Bathurst, 22 December 1826, *H.R.A.*, I, xii, p. 796.

Do you allude to the difference of civilization?—No; the wretchedness of their appearance, and the diseases with which they were evidently infected.

More in the vicinity of towns than in the country?—Much more in the vicinity of towns that in the country; there was a healthiness about the appearance of the country natives that was not to be found in those living within a few miles of the large towns.

To what do you ascribe such deterioration?—To the demoralizing influence which the convicts of New South Wales principally, and some of the settlers have upon the natives.

Are the aborigines there generally in a very miserable and degraded state?—Very miserable and degraded; much below the New Zealanders.

And yet you describe those in the vicinity of Sydney to be still more debased in their condition and habits?—Still more debased; resulting I should certainly say, from the connexion they have had with Europeans.[28]

> The Rev. J.S.C. Handt, in Sydney waiting for his companions to arrive from England before proceeding to Wellington Valley, saw that the Aborigines were capable of imitating the better aspects of European civilization, yet had absorbed only the vices.

122 The Aborigines that walk here about the streets of Sydney are, I am sorry to say, initiated in all European vices. It is indeed time that the blessings of the Gospel should be known to them, after they have been greatly deprived of their country, their hunting and fishing places, and made the children of hell by the Europeans ten times more than they were before. Especially as they are capable of learning to perform any European business and of improving their intellects.[29]

The Aboriginal view of things

> Evidence of the way Aborigines viewed the white men and their culture is not easily found. Clearly, any comments made by the natives would have had to have been recorded by white men, and as these comments may often have been derogatory it is perhaps understandable that not many survive. The most valuable source of Aboriginal opinion is the journals of the missionaries. These men often recorded conversations they had with natives, generally with the object of showing the inferiority of the latter, but usually at the same time revealing Aboriginal attitudes.
>
> The two following extracts demonstrate that the Aborigines were able to find flaws in European teaching:

---

[28] Select Committee on Aborigines (British Settlements) 1835, *B.P.P.*, Vol. VII, p. 201.
[29] Handt to C.M.S. London, 30 September 1831, C.M.S. microfilmed archives.

123 Cochran told me "I must go to the Camp, the Old Men make me go". What need you care, I replied, for these old wicked fellows: he significantly rejoined "Why you care for the Governor. These old men our Governors we must do what they say". We are certain as observation has so frequently taught us that if it were not for the elderly Natives who will continue in their wild heathen habits we should do far better with the young generation.[30]

> An Aboriginal woman had been caught in the act of killing her half-caste baby. She and her blind husband were staying temporarily at the Wellington Valley Mission.

124 I spoke this morning with the blind husband, and reproved him for having prostituted his wife. He replied that white men should know that it was wrong and not have asked her of him, as they knew about God &c. A just reply indeed. Those who should endeavour to teach them good things, render them by their conduct and conversation worse than they were before.[31]

> The following recorded conversation would suggest that the Aborigines were confident that they had as much to teach white men as they had to learn from them.

125 Goongeen. "Have you ever seen something like stars fall? That always come down when black fellow going to die."
Mr. Watson. "Pshaw! Not so, I think."
G. "Hy, hy, hy! You won't believe black fellow: black fellow won't believe you."[32]

> Nor were they beyond questioning the logic of Christian teaching.

126 A few days ago Mr. Therry, one of the Romish Priests baptized some infant black natives, and upon informing the parents and others, that after death they would all rise again, one of them said, "If black man jump again, what for bury him?"[33]

> One small piece of evidence suggests that the natives were not necessarily impressed by the continual preaching of the missionaries. Some Aborigines asked a Mr Fisher for tobacco, and were told to go to the Wellington Mission to get some.

127 "Oh no," they replied; "too much Mr Watson pyhalla (a vulgar word for 'to speak'). "That fellow always pyhalla. We don't want pyhalla: we want tobacco, pipes, bread."[34]

---

[30] James Günther, Journal, 1836–65, 7 August 1838, M.L. MSS. B504.
[31] J. S. C. Handt, Journal, 28 April 1833, C.M.S. microfilmed archives.
[32] W. Watson, Journal, 26 April 1834, *C.M.S. Missionary Register*, 1835, p. 519.
[33] Lawry to Wesleyan Committee, 1 June 1821, Bonwick Transcripts, Box 51, M.L.
[34] W. Watson, Journal, 16 March 1834, *C.M.S. Missionary Register*, 1835, p. 517.

Some insight into the Aboriginal view of agricultural pursuits comes to us through the missionaries.

128   When speaking to Goongeen to-day respecting some of the wheat in the paddock where he is working, it being his own, he said, "What shall I do with it? Directly black fellow know I got wheat, they come up, and eat it up all at once; and then I shall have to go into the bush, like another black fellow." There was much truth in his remarks; and in them may be perceived one of the impediments that lie in the way of their becoming possessed of property.[35]

Threlkeld had had the same sort of response at Reid's Mistake.

129   Unless the Government afford such protection as will prevent their ferocious attacks upon each other, it is impossible to retain any party in one place for a length of time. On requesting McGill [an Aborigine] to plant corn on a piece of ground which I had prepared for him, his reply was, "It would be useless, as the tribes from the neighbouring Sugar Loaf Mountain, would come down and take it away when ripe, although on friendly terms". The whole system of the blacks, is that of continued aggressions against each other, which, whilst it is opposed to every effort, or exertion to civilize them, demonstrates the necessity of Christian instruction, which alone can change their habits of life.[36]

The attitude of the Aborigines towards manual labour is manifested in the two following quotations, and an implied amusement at the Europeans' zeal for work can be detected.

130   Asked one native why didn't cultivate ground and have plenty to eat. Said, "it was too warm to work." Asked whether too warm to eat when he could get white man's food. He then began to laugh, and said he would work by and by.[37]

One of the Aborigines, who often visits us, was asked, whether he would work a little for us: he replied in the negative; and the reason he assigned for the refusal was, because he was full up. Thus, as he was not hungry, he thought it unreasonable to work. But that is their way of thinking and doing.[38]

Sometimes the families of the missionaries were abused. Handt's children were frequently the victims of Aboriginal naughtiness.

---

[35] 7 July 1836, *ibid.*, 1838, p. 424.
[36] Threlkeld in evidence before the Committee on the Aborigines Question, *N.S.W.L.C.V.P.*, 1838, p. 21.
[37] J. S. C. Handt, Journal, *C.M.S. Missionary Register*, 1834, p. 153.
[38] J. S. C. Handt, Journal, 22 May 1840, C.M.S. microfilmed archives.

131   The Aboriginal boys are becoming insolent at present, finding fault with the victuals given them, frequently hurting our children, and becoming very rude and insulting to ourselves.[39]

An Aboriginal Boy came to our window to-day; but because I could not attend to him the very moment he made his appearance, he went to our little Ambrose, who was playing outside by himself, and dirtied his hat all over, and then ran away.[40]

> The amusement with which the Aboriginal children regarded their lessons was a source of regret to the Missionaries, but gives us a glimpse of Aboriginal attitudes.

132   They were much amused when repeating the numbers, and made a kind of song of them, by singing them out, and beating time with their womeras. They received some biscuit after they had asked a blessing in their own language. When they had gone out, they were heard to repeat part of it again, and to laugh heartily; poor creatures.[41]

> It is interesting to note that the European blanket, for long considered the universal palliative for all native ills, was in fact, regarded by the natives as a makeshift inferior to their own opossum skin cloaks; and other European clothes were not greatly appreciated by the Aborigines. They did not want them.

133   A certain number amongst them may have learned to adopt for a time, if not fully appreciate the convenience of European clothing. The blanket, the slop clothing of the shepherd, or the cast off suit of the townsman, may be seen, in certain instances, to supersede for a time the opossum skin cloak, which forms almost the only garment of the Aboriginal Native in the state of nature. But the blanket as a garment has less power than the native opossum cloak, to resist either cold or heat, or the wear and tear of the scrub. It is further easily disposed of; and the temptation to such disposal is not wanting. The superior comfort of the more perfect European clothing is supported. It may be appreciated in so far as an approximation to the customs of the white man be considered advantageous, or flatter the vanity of the Native. But I question whether any number of instances can be cited of its complete and permanent adoption, from a conviction of its superior comfort and decency. The fact is, both by male and female, it is thrown aside without ceremony, as soon as circumstances tempt or permit.[42]

[39] *Ibid.*, 3 February 1839.
[40] *Ibid.*, 11 September 1840.
[41] *Ibid.*, 20 December 1838.
[42] La Trobe to Thomson, 18 November 1848, Appendix to Report from Select Committee on the Aborigines and Protectorate, *N.S.W.L.C.V.P.*, 1849, p. 5.

5
The Public Conscience

The preceding two chapters have been concerned with the bitterness and antagonisms that developed between the Aborigines and the whites. Yet, as we saw in Chapter 2, not all whites treated the natives with contempt, and some made positive attempts to ameliorate their condition. This chapter will show the existence of a public conscience in the colony. This conscience was largely expressed in the newspapers and journals of the day and in the several public enquiries into the condition of Aborigines.

It is interesting to see how frequently the columns of the *Sydney Gazette* were devoted to the plight of the Aborigines, in marked contrast to the hostility sometimes expressed by other papers, such as the *Australian*—examples of which were quoted in Chapter 3.

One of the earliest recorded observations made by a white man who saw the Aborigines' condition in a sympathetic light, appeared in Captain Watkin Tench's book, first published in 1789. Chiding those who despised the Aborigines as inferior beings, Tench wrote:

134   . . . let those who have been born in more favoured lands, and who have profited by more enlightened systems, compassionate, but not despise, their destitute and obscure situation. Children of the same omniscient paternal care, let them recollect, that by fortuitous advantage of birth alone, they possess superiority: that untaught, unaccommodated man, is the same in Pall Mall, as in the wilderness of New South Wales: and ultimately let them hope, and trust, that the progress of reason, and the splendor of revelation, will in their proper and allotted season, be permitted to illumine, and transfuse into these desert regions, knowledge, virtue, and happiness.[1]

Writing to Dr A. Clarke in London, the Rev. S. Leigh saw the Native School founded by Governor Macquarie as the only hope for the rapidly dying race.

135   This is the only plan from which we may expect any degree of Civillisation—I am informed that the native parents diminish in

---

[1] Watkin Tench, *Sydney's First Four Years, being a reprint of A Narrative of the Expedition to Botany Bay and A Complete Account of the Settlement at Port Jackson* [1789 and 1793], Sydney, 1961, pp. 293-4.

number, that there is not half the number that there was 20 years since. The cause is attributed to the want of food and an avertion to industry.[2]

> 'Philanthropus' wrote frequently to the *Sydney Gazette* on the subject of the Aborigines. As his name suggests, he favoured a friendly approach. Indeed, he claimed the Australian natives as brothers.

136 I suppose the New Hollanders to be *human creatures*, and that their Maker has taught them more than the beasts of the earth. I think they have with myself, and all other men, one *common ancestor*. I am therefore willing to call them brethren, and to acknowledge them entitled to my compassion and fraternal respect. Hence, I have been led to estimate *even* the least one of these, my despised and injured brethren, at more value than all the sheep and cattle on Bathurst Plains; than all the flocks and herds in the territory of New South Wales; than all the animals in the whole world!

In the sight of the *Creator*, their souls I believe to be of infinite importance. . . . If we therefore now hasten their destruction, or neglect to promote their salvation, shall we be innocent, or without blame?[3]

> The above extract is taken from a letter in answer to 'Fidelis', who had written demanding the immediate punishment of Aborigines who had attacked shepherds and stock-keepers, 'our fellow subjects'. 'Fidelis', in turn, replied to 'Philanthropus' through the medium of the same journal. He claimed that it was all very well for 'Philanthropus' to make such claims from the comfort of his own fireside; the blacks had been the aggressors and no Europeans had robbed them of towns or villages:

137 I never denied the fact of the Aborigines being our fellow creatures, but I *feel* sensibly, that human nature should appear in so deteriorated a state, incapable of any reformation. All attempts have hitherto proven unsatisfactory, with the additional assurance of determined innate treachery, accompanying the most earnest endeavours. No race were ever so distinguished for ignorance and heathenish barbarity, or that merited less interest.[4]

> With the arrival of Archdeacon Broughton (later to become the Bishop of Australia), the future of the Aborigines appeared to some to be brighter. The Archdeacon had requested his clergy to furnish him with any information that could assist him in his work with the natives, and the *Gazette* emulated him, calling for advice from its readers.

[2] Leigh to Clarke, 14 October 1817, Bonwick Transcripts, Box 50, M.L.
[3] *Sydney Gazette*, 5 August 1824.
[4] *Ibid.*, 19 August 1824.

138   It will be observed that the Venerable the ARCHDEACON is determined on sparing no exertions for the instruction of the Aborigines. It is HIS MAJESTY'S gracious and declared wish, that this duty should be diligently attended to by his Australian subjects; and having the KING for their patron, and the Clergy for their coadjutors, we do hope the people will cheerfully co-operate in this just but truly difficult undertaking. What is most wanted at the present moment, are the opinions of intelligent men as to the most promising way in which the operations should be commenced. The failure, or at all events the comparative inefficiency, of the attempts hitherto made, points out the necessity of a careful survey of the wilderness it is proposed to cultivate, that we may know where to select the best spot to begin with, and how we may employ our limited means to the greatest possible advantage. Acting on this precautionary rule, the ARCHDEACON has called upon the Clergy for their individual opinions and suggestions; and in furtherance of the same preliminary object, we beg to invite from our intelligent readers a communication of the sentiments they may have formed on the subject. Many of them, we know, have regarded the Blacks as an interesting subject of curiosity, and attentively studied the peculiarities of their character and customs. From such persons many useful hints might be derived, and we trust they will favour the public, through the medium of our columns, with the result of their speculations.[5]

Within a fortnight of this appeal, they published extracts from the Archdeacon's Charge to the Clergy:

139   The last subject with which I shall at present detain you, is the condition of the native or aboriginal inhabitants of this country. It is an awful, it is even an appalling consideration, that after an intercourse of nearly half a century with a Christian people, these hapless human beings continue to this day in the original benighted and degraded state. I may even proceed farther; so far as to express my fears that our settlement in their country has even deteriorated a condition of existence, than which, before our interference, nothing more miserable could easily be conceived. While, as the contagion of European intercourse has extended itself among them, they gradually lose the better properties of their own character, they appear in exchange to acquire none but the most objectionable and degrading of ours. The most revolting spectacle which presents itself to a stranger newly arriving on these

---

[5] *Ibid.*, 21 January 1830.

shores, is the sight of their natural occupants reduced to a state of worse than barbarian wildness by that fondness for intoxicating liquors which they imbibed from our example; and in reckless addiction to which they are still encouraged by many whose superiority in knowledge ought to have been directed to some less unchristian purpose. But can we satisfy ourselves, my brethren, that we have fulfilled all our duty while such a spectacle is exhibited before us? Shall we look on and see them perish, without so much as an effort for their preservation? Natural and much more Christian equity points out that as in the occupation of their soil we are partakers of their worldly things, so in justice should they be of our spiritual. As through the tender mercy of our God the day spring from on high has visited us, we are solemnly engaged to impart to them the glorious beams of Gospel truth to guide their feet into the way of peace.

I am aware of attempts having been undertaken with this view, and of their abandonment from a sense of existing difficulties and despair of final success. But from the very nature of the undertaking obstacles were to be anticipated. Every advancement of the Christian religion, from its first origin to this day, has been effected in opposition to difficulties which, in a natural sense, might be termed insuperable. Its excellency and its derivation from a heavenly source have been best demonstrated by surmounting such opposition. It may be considered after all a very doubtful question whether the erratic habits and inconsiderate disposition of the native tribes are in reality more adverse to the reception of Christianity than those propensities which its earliest preachers had to encounter in the nations they addressed; the obstinate superstitution of the Jew, and the philosophic arrogance of the Gentile. But suppose them to be so, what shall we say? Shall we therefore desist? Unhesitatingly I answer, No. Persevere as you regard the honour of God, and as you value the souls of these your helpless and unhappy fellow creatures. The very ground which we tread upon, teaches us this lesson. What does it exhibit but the sublime spectacle of the triumph of civilized man over the ruggedness of the physical world? And shall the Christian philantrophist despair of having, in God's good time, an equal right to rejoice in the success of his exertions to produce a moral reform, and by spiritual cultivation to reclaim that human wilderness which extends on every side of us? The feeling which I derive from difficulties in such a case, and would communicate to those around me, is animation not despair. God works in every dispensation for his own glory, and in his own foreordained times and seasons; and his purpose in permitting the existence of such difficulties may be to furnish an immediate exercise of our faith and patience, and, in their final subjugation, a clearer manifestation of his own Omnipotence.[6]

The *Gazette* devoted the editorial of the same issue to comments on this Charge.

140 In another column we give copious extracts from the ARCHDEACON'S Charge, on the subject of our duty, as a Colony of Britons and of Christians, to better the condition of the Aborigines. We are perfectly aware of the objections usually brought forward against any such attempt. One of them is, that they are happy enough in their present state, and that our interference with their established habits would be an unnecessary disturbance of their repose—

> "Where ignorance is bliss,
> 'Twere folly to be wise."

This proposition is essentially the same with those old-fashioned prejudices against the education of the lower orders, which the present diffusion of knowledge puts to open shame. If the New Hollanders are *men*—and who would be hardy enough to deny their claim to our common nature?—then does it follow as a clear consequence, that they are as much injured by the want of civilization, and would be as extensively benefited by its bestowment, as any other part of the family of man. If the relapse of the British isles into their primitive barbarism would be deprecated as the worst of calamaties, on what rational principle can it be maintained, that with other portions of mankind barbarism is a state which it were cruel to reform? If the New Hollander would be the worse for cultivation, then the Ancient Britons were a more enviable race than the present enlightened occupants of their soil; and instead of founding schools and colleges, in imitation of the modern example of British history, we should be rendering a kindlier service to the youth of Australia, by debarring them from the fountains of knowledge, and holding up the Blacks as the teachers best qualified to guide them to contentment and happiness! But it is a waste of time to combat sophisms so hollow and heartless. Barbarism *is not* and *never was* a state of happiness: its pleasures are little better than those of the oyster, contracted, sensual, and monotonous, altogether beneath the high endowments and illimitable capacities of our nature; it is a collapsion of those faculties the exercise of which leads to the purest, and richest, and most lasting enjoyments; a condition, in short, which no civilized man can contemplate without an

---

[6] *Ibid.*, 4 February 1830.

exalted sense of his own superiority in all the properties of a rational and a happy existence. And if the Blacks of this country are indeed, to use the quaint language of Shakespeare,

"Imbued with intellectual sense and souls,
Of more pre-eminence than fish and fowls,"

it is mere trifling to talk of the cruelty of disturbing the torpor of their barbarism.

But the most plausible objection, and we allow it to be a very serious one, is the failure of all past efforts to train them to permanent civilized habits. It should, however, be borne in mind, that those efforts have been chiefly confined to individuals; and even where they have been combined, as in Governor MACQUARIE'S Institution, they have wanted that studious attention to the native language, that undaunted perseverance in the face of difficulties and disappointments, and that following up of the system to its final practical results, without which real success cannot be reasonably looked for.

The ARCHDEACON, as we stated some time ago, has already begun to act, and has entered upon his work at the right end—the acquirement of the language. To the Rev. Mr. THRELKELD, who has got the start in this department of the undertaking, the Venerable Gentleman, in conjunction with others, has extended a liberal encouragement; and if the persons about to be stationed in several parts of the Colony for the same purpose, devote themselves with as much spirit as Mr. T. to the study of the native tongue, it will not be long before we shall be able to open Native Schools with the necessary apparatus of grammars, vocabularies, and other elementary books.

We cannot conclude without expressing the gratification we experience, in seeing, in so high a functionary, a warm and active friend to the poor, despised, and deeply-injured Black.[7]

It seemed that those who tried to help the Aborigines had to remind themselves and others constantly, that these people were *human*.

141   It would afford us peculiar satisfaction to be enabled to record even one instance of conversion to Christianity among this benighted race; but alas! so far as our observation has extended, they do not appear, in our opinion, to exercise either gratitude or reflection. However, with all their moral degredation and apparent small degree of superiority to the brute creation, we believe that they are men, and, as such, are interested in the economy of sal-

---

[7] *Ibid.*, (On Threlkeld, see Chapter 6.)

vation. Under such views, we feel it our duty to labour to instruct them in the great things of God.[8]

Drastic steps to solve the apparent decline of the natives were suggested by Lt R. Sadlier, R.N., Master of the Male Orphan School at Liverpool, before the Committee on the Aborigines Question:

142 Those within the pale of white population must within a very few years, be utterly destroyed, if the most prompt measures be not taken—so much so, that I conceive that there is scarce an alternative between coercion and destruction. I would therefore beg to recommend a clause to be introduced into the Vagrant Act, empowering their transportation, under peculiar circumstances, to distant parts of the colony—say Moreton Bay, Port Phillip, &c.; it being a well known fact, that when sent to a distance, they can be made to work; and from their great apprehension of strange tribes, their erratic habits can be restrained.[9]

The same Committee received a letter from the Rev. W. M. Cowper to the Bishop of Australia:

143 It is certainly the duty of the British Government and of the colony to do all in their power to preserve this unhappy race from extirpation, and not to leave them in a worse condition than that in which they previously existed. But more than this, they ought not to be satisfied with any thing less than making them Christians, and elevating them to that scale in human society, for which they may be fitted by instruction and civilization, and to which Christianity will eventually lead them.[10]

One example of the growing concern about the condition of the Aborigines was the founding of an Australian Aborigines Protection Society in 1838.

144 A meeting of gentlemen interested in the welfare of the Aboriginal inhabitants of this territory was held at the house of the Rev. J. Saunders, in Prince Street, on Monday evening last, to consider the propriety of adopting some means for bettering the condition of these miserable children of the forest. The Rev. Dr. Lang was called to the chair, and a series of resolutions entered into for the formation of a Society for the protection and advancement of the Aborigines of this colony, and the adjacent islands, in connexion with the British and Foreign Aborigines Protection Society.

---

[8] William Watson quoted in *C.M.S. Missionary Register* for 1834, p. 504.
[9] Evidence before the 1838 Committee on the Aborigines Question, *N.S.W.L.C.V.P.*, 1838, pp. 31–2.
[10] *Ibid.*, p. 60.

This new benevolent association is to be called the Australian Aborigines Protection Society. . . .[11]

> The Committee consisted of four clergymen, the director of the male orphan institution, the Chief Protector of Aborigines and three Assistant Protectors, and five leading settlers.
> Another Select Committee on the condition of Aborigines was held in 1845, and Polding, the Roman Catholic Bishop, gave evidence. Some of his suggestions harked back to the ideas put forward by Governor Macquarie thirty years earlier.

145   I conceive if the Government were to take care of the aborigines, and give them tracts of land on which they might congregate, and where they would be in safety, much good might be done, even in the civilized parts of the Colony. They might be encouraged to have little gardens, and be gradually brought into habits of civilization. Beyond the boundaries, the only way would be to allot to them certain portions of ground, to let them have cattle and other things for their use. Instead of protectors with large salaries, industrious simple minded married men might have the care of them, to prevent the intrusion of the Whites, and to look after their well being and concerns. The natives would soon learn that it was better to tend their cattle, and to be able to kill an ox when they required it, than to hunt the kangaroo or emu. The natives would have confidence inspired by the fact that they would have an asylum where they would be safe from the aggressions of the Whites.[12]

> It is clear that the Bishop believed 'civilization' of the Aborigines to be possible, if approached the right way.

146   Then, in the first instance [he was asked], you think you must attend to their physical wants? Undoubtedly; thus you conciliate confidence, induce moral habits, give expansion to the mental powers, thus you prepare them for religious truths. It must be proved to the savage that the White man is his kind friend; that if he drives away the food natural to the country, he provides better; that he has the well being of the aborigines at heart; and that, if it is necessary for the purposes of civilized life, to occupy his land, it is not taken away without remuneration and reciprocal advantage. If the Whites could also be impressed with the grievous impropriety of making use of the women of the aborigines, as they are used, the way would be opened for them doing much good; and I have not the

---

[11] *Colonist*, 3 October 1838.
[12] *N.S.W.L.C.V.P.*, 1845, p. 9.

least doubt that the aborigines of this Colony might be brought into a high state of civilization.[13]

Another witness put forward a solution which had been suggested by the very early settlers, including Marsden.

147 In my opinion it is impossible to persuade the men to give up their wandering life, but by taking the children from them very young, and bringing them up in an establishment where they would have no opportunity of seeing any but Europeans, they would, I have no doubt, become useful members of society, and their condition would be much improved. The parents could be easily persuaded to give up their children, and the number of children in this district is so small, that the expense would be but trifling.[14]

Replying to a request to give the Committee any facts that would assist in the promotion of the Aborigines' welfare, D. Dunlop Esq., J.P., suggested that whites must be reformed first:

148 Their eternal welfare ought to be the first of all things cared for, but this onerous task, I fear, can only be accomplished when there shall be a thorough reformation in the white population, for while reckless men, and abandoned women, ignorant of divine, and despising all human laws, are living examples daily before them, the aborigines cannot learn to love or venerate our laws, our customs, or our religion. Less than six years ago, in this district, the Sabbath was as all the other days of the week; killing and salting meat, making butter, baking, washing, and reaping, and carting home grain, were as sedulously followed, as if a day of rest had never been ordained by the Almighty, and this not alone by the lowest order of settlers, but by those having large establishments, and being the assignees of numerous convicts. Even yet, we have not a resident minister of the Gospel nearer than thirty-five miles, but within the past year, a pious teacher of the Wesleyan faith has brought many souls into the paths of godliness, and already our aborigines begin to count their time by Sundays, when "day him no work". The Committee can best promote the welfare of the aborigines by enforcing on the minds of those who have the power, the necessity of sending the word of God to our homes in the wilderness, and furnishing us with the good examples of Christian ministers and their families....[15]

[13] *Ibid.*, p. 10.
[14] Evidence of W. N. Gray, Esq., J.P., Police Magistrate of Port Macquarie, *ibid.*, p. 26.
[15] *Ibid.*, p. 31.

The growth of the public conscience had come, by the 1840s, the full circle to where the Rev. Richard Johnson had pinpointed the problem in 1792. It seemed impossible to do anything about the Aborigines when they were surrounded by the vicious examples of the whites. The Rev. Dr J. D. Lang speculated on the possible effect on the Aborigines of a settlement not consisting of convicts:

149 Whether the condition of the native inhabitants of New South Wales would have been improved, had their territory been seized by Europeans of the average character of the inhabitants of Britain, may admit of question. Decidedly averse to amalgamate with Europeans, or to embrace the habits of European civilization, the occupation of their hunting-grounds, and the clearing away of their native forests, in which the kangaroos and opossums find shelter and subsistence, would certainly have diminished their means of supporting animal life, even in the best possible circumstances in which such a settlement could have been effected, and would therefore have tended rather to deteriorate than to ameliorate their condition; for the state of miserable dependence on European charity, which in such circumstances uniformly supersedes their natural state of salutary dependence on their own resources, is but a poor substitute for the manlier energies and the other minor virtues of savage life, and perhaps tends, more than anything else, to thin the ranks of the dispirited aborigines, and to hasten their entire disappearance from the face of colonial society.

But if such would have been the condition of the aborigines of New South Wales, even in the most favourable circumstances in which a British colony could have been formed in their territory, how greatly aggravated must have been the evils of their actual condition, as a race of savages, living in contact with a community of civilized men, when the latter consisted for the most part of the off-scourings of all things; and how rapidly must the progress of the wretched aborigines have been accelerated to moral degradation and utter extinction! In short, the condition of the aborigines of New South Wales and Van Diemen's Land, ever since the first settlement of these colonies, has been peculiarly unfortunate, and calls loudly for the beneficent interference of the Imperial Legislature in their behalf. Their hunting-grounds have been seized by Europeans, and the kangaroos have accordingly disappeared from their wonted fields, and the opposums from the fallen trees of their ancient forests. But what compensation have they received for their loss of all things that are held valuable by savage man? What equivalent has been afforded them in exchange for their fields and their forests? Why, the very worst features of English civilization have re-appeared in their territory. They have been transformed into a race of paupers, and taught to beg their bread where they formerly earned it. Their native habits of temperance have been succeeded by scenes of beastly intoxication. Their tongues have been taught to frame horrid imprecations in a language which they imperfectly understand. Their bodies have been wasted by strange and incurable diseases. Their impatience of injuries has been tried with the most wanton and brutal aggressions, and in moments of frenzy they have sometimes been stimulated to deeds of indiscriminate and murderous revenge.[16]

---

[16] Lang to T. F. Buxton, 10 June 1834, in evidence to Select Committee on Aborigines (British Settlements), *B.P.P.* Vol. VII, p. 682.

6

The Work of the Missionaries

The First Attempt: Wesleyans Walker and Harper

One of the recurring themes of previous chapters has been that of converting the Aborigines to Christianity. Many believed that this would be the only way to 'civilize' them and to make them 'fit' members of a British form of society. Missions were undertaken by most of the major denominations. The evangelical stress on industry played a large part in this desire to convert the natives, for they appeared excessively idle in the eyes of Europeans. Their nakedness, their lack of houses, their failure to cultivate the soil, all pointed to the need for the disciplines of Christianity.

Of course, there were those Englishmen who wanted to bring to the heathen Christianity for its own sake, rather than for its civilizing 'side-effects'. Even before the first fleet left England, the Rev. H. Venn was highly optimistic about the future held out to the Aborigines by Christianity. In a letter to his daughter, in which he saw New Holland as a place where the convicts would be no longer lost creatures, he also saw a bright future for the natives of that land.

150   ... With what pleasure may we consider this plan of peopling that far distant region, and other opening connexions with the Heathen, as a foundation for the Gospel of our God and Saviour to be preached unto them;—when "a vast multitude, whom no man can number", shall "call upon his Name";—When "the wilderness shall become a fruitful field", and all the savageness of the Heathen shall be put off, and all the graces of the Spirit shall be put on.[1]

However, no missionaries were sent out specifically to work among the Aborigines for some time. Some of the colonial clergy and missionaries sent to the South Seas in the 1790s investigated the possibilities of missions to the Aborigines, but not all were optimistic.

151   In our letters by the *Barwell*, we expressed some hopes of being able to do Something here among the Natives; but at that

---

[1] Rev. H. Venn to his daughter, 28 October 1786, Bonwick Transcripts, Box 49, M.L.

time we knew but little about their manner of life, customs & dispositions, & a variety of circumstances which render our being useful to them impracticable, yet I might say almost impossible at present. I cannot enter into particulars concerning them now, but shall, Godwilling, Some other opportunity of writing.[2]

> The first person to be appointed as a missionary to the Aborigines was the Rev. William Walker, who came to the colony in 1821 under the auspices of the Wesleyan Missionary Society. Within a very short time of his arrival he wrote to his society in London:

152 Let me add, what you do, do quickly. These poor creatures are dying from cold and nakedness, and famine. The bare mentioning of which is sufficient to raise every tender feeling in your heart. It was an observation of the Governor's that will never lose its impression on my mind; that authorized me to write this paragraph. "If something is not done" says His Excellency "for these poor, distressed creatures, they will become extinct: the race of them will perish from absolute want!"[3]

> William Walker and the Rev. W. Lawry (also a Wesleyan) waited upon the newly arrived Governor Brisbane, who expressed interest in the mission to the Aborigines. Lawry wrote to the London headquarters of his society, describing his talk with Brisbane:

153 ... and said he traveled much among savages in America and else where, and consequently knew much of the manners and capabilities—the present was a glorious epoch when the British people were zealous and successful in reclaiming great numbers of these poor creatures, in America and Africa; he had read our Report while on the passage, and was very much pleased to see what good we were doing.[4]

> Alas for the Governor's optimism, the 'glorious epoch' was not to appear in his time, or indeed at all. The story of the missions is a long one, and space permits only a brief examination of the aims, of the achievements and of the failures. Certainly there was no immediate success with the arrival of Walker, a man specially appointed to minister to the Aborigines. He had been in the Colony only a few weeks before he decided that he needed an assistant.

154 From the wandering habits of the Aborigines, it appears, that the presence of another Missionary is indispensable. The itineracy to which I must submit, will render the presence of another brother at the settlement too apparently necessary, to be presented

---

[2] William Henry to London Missionary Society, 29 August 1799, *ibid.*
[3] Walker to Rev. W. Watson, 17 October 1821, *ibid.*, Box 51.
[4] Lawry to General Committee Wesleyan Missionary Society, 19 November 1821, *ibid.*, Box 52.

to you under the garb of plausible language. The natives must have some person with them to encourage, to instruct, and to persuade.[5]

The C.M.S. Register for 1822 reported the appointment of Walker. Again there was an air of optimism:

155   The case of the wretched men has been laid on the hearts of the pious in the Colony; and earnest appeals have been made in their behalf, with a view of producing a systematic effort for the religious instruction; and, in consequence, some means have been adopted for that purpose. With those who have thus commenced this benevolent work, Mr. Walker is instructed to co-operate, and to follow any plans which may appear most conducive to this end. His first effort will be among those who lie nearest the Settlements, whose children especially he will endeavour to bring under a course of useful and religious instruction.[6]

In spite of Walker's attempts, and those of John Harper who joined the Wesleyan Mission to the Aborigines, no successes could be reported. Four years after Walker's arrival the *Gazette* could only talk about the continued degradation of the natives.

156   The continued degradation of these tribes, that live within the precints of the Colony, not withstanding the many years that they have witnessed the refinements and advantages of civilization, shew that they will never spontaneously abandon their barbarous habits and apply themselves to useful industry, and that this change in their character cannot be effected without bringing them under the controul of direct persevering instruction and discipline.[7]

The local branch of the Wesleyan Society, in reporting to their London headquarters, blamed the nomadic life of the Aborigines for the failure of the mission.

157   What to say or write about Mr. Walker's Mission—the poor fellow, has not been idle in his Colonial Mission he has laboured and that with some success; in his Black Mission he has done what he could. They are a most trying uncertain people, and their prediliction in favour of a wandering life greatly tends to keep them ignorant and miserable. . . . To form an establishment and keep them together w^d be very expensive, . . . I really hope we shall hear from you in reference to the aborigines of N.S.W.[8]

---

[5] Walker to Watson, 12 October 1821, *ibid.*, Box 51.
[6] *C.M.S. Missionary Register*, 1822, p. 92.
[7] *Sydney Gazette*, 29 September 1825.
[8] Erskine to Watson, 23 October 1823, Bonwick Transcripts, Box 52, M.L.

Threlkeld and the Language

The idea of settling the natives in reserved areas was not new, as we have seen in Governor Macquarie's time, and in 1825 10,000 acres of land at Reid's Mistake, near Lake Macquarie, were set aside by the Governor for a native settlement. A missionary of the London Missionary Society was appointed to work among them. He was the Rev. Lancelot Threlkeld, a man with missionary experience in the Friendly Islands. Writing to the Rev. George Burder, Secretary of the L.M.S., Threlkeld indicated that there was some opposition in the Colony to an Aboriginal Mission.

158   It is my intention to act here upon the same plan we found so successful at Raiatea namely, Give nothing to any individual but in return for some labor for common good. There is nothing to flatter sanguine expectations in the beginning of this Mission—It is a thing spoken against, as impracticable by every one. But to the Christian who views by faith it is one of those mountains that shall become a plain, or be cast into the sea.[9]

Threlkeld devoted a great part of his time to acquiring the language of the Aborigines at Reid's Mistake, compiling a grammar, and translating the Bible. Most of his knowledge of the language was derived from working with the natives.

159   The natives were now employed in falling trees and burning off, so as to clear a portion of land for the cultivation of Indian corn and wheat; we supplying them for their labour with food and slops, tobacco and fish-hooks. They worked well whilst under the direction of a free man and his two sons, . . . each one taking a certain number of Aborigines as his gang of workmen; myself being among them amidst surrounding fires, and under a vertical sun, with my book, collecting words and phrases, and endeavouring to converse with them in their own tongue.[10]

Threlkeld also accompanied the natives on hunting excursions with his book and pencil. His concentration on their language was part of a long-term plan to Christianize them.

160   With respect to seeing my system, it can be seen and known in two minutes, namely, first obtain the language, then preach the Gospel, then urge them from Gospel motives to be industrious, at the same time becoming a servant to them to win them to that which is right.[11]

[9] Threlkeld to Burder, 2 February 1825, *ibid.*, Box 53.
[10] L. E. Threlkeld, *A Statement chiefly relating to the formation and Abandonment of a Mission to the Aborigines of New South Wales;* . . . Sydney, 1828, p. 11.
[11] Threlkeld to Attorney-General Saxe Bannister, September 1825, Bonwick Transcripts, Box 53, M.L.

However, Threlkeld soon came into collision with the London Missionary Society over his heavy expenditure, and the Society refused to honour bills he had drawn in their name. When the missionary was taken to Court, the *Sydney Gazette* was one journal which leapt to his defence.

161 We are extremely sorry to understand, that the Rev. Mr. THRELKELD, the London Missionary Society, has been reluctantly induced to abandon his Mission-station at Reid's Mistake, after the most indefatigable pains to secure the language, and promote the professed views of the Society to which Mr. THRELKELD belongs... [he] relinquished his former sphere of extensive usefulness in the Society Isles—and entered upon a new and more complicated scene of Ministerial duty, in which success was beginning to succeed the most elaborate exertions, when, lo and behold! for the sake of a paltry hundred or two hundred a-year, the Mission— which embraces the moral and eternal condition of three millions of the human race—is abondoned! Mr. THRELKELD, however, as he intends to reside in Sydney for the purpose of proceeding in the acquirement of the aboriginal language, shows that he is determined to prosecute his labours at some future period, when the London Committee grow wiser, and allow their Missionaries the privilege of thinking and acting, as circumstances may dictate, and not be bandied about by men who may possess intelligence and piety in abundance, but still be as ignorant concerning the local condition of the people amongst whom their Missionaries are called to act, as the Emporer of Morocco is acquainted with the Liberty of the Press, or Magna Carta.[12]

Other journals were no less verbose in the condemnation of Threlkeld. For a time the Mission seemed in danger of collapse, but eventually the local authorities came to Threlkeld's aid. He summed up his experiences in his evidence before the 1838 Committee on the Aborigines Question.

162 I reside at Lake Macquarie, and have done so nearly fourteen years, during which I have been engaged in acquiring a knowledge of the language of the Aboriginal natives, and instructing them; for six years of that period, my undertaking was carried on under the auspices of the London Missionary Society; but owing to the heavy expense of the Mission, amounting to about £500 per annum for my own support, and that of such natives as I could persuade to remain with me, for the double purpose of obtaining from them a knowledge of their language, and to give me an opportunity of endeavouring to civilize and instruct them. The Society being disappointed in the amount of aid expected from other quarters,

[12] *Sydney Gazette*, 8 October 1827.

and regarding the expense as encroaching too much upon their funds, relinquished the Mission, and for nearly two years I was left to my own resources, and the assistance of some friends, without other aid, when General Darling obtained the authority of the Secretary of State, for an allowance of £150 a year, and £36 in lieu of rations for four convict servants, which has been granted to me during the last eight years.[13]

In spite of his years of work and the expenditure of vast sums of money, Threlkeld could claim little success in converting the Aborigines to Christianity or in encouraging them to settle down to a life of agriculture.

163 With respect to *the mission of the Rev. Mr. Threlkeld, at Lake Macquarie*, it would seem, from the final report of that gentleman to the government, in which he sketches the history of his engagements amongst the blacks during the period of seventeen years, that the plan of operations pursued by him was mainly directed to the acquirement of their language—the compilation of a grammar thereof—and the translation of various parts of Scripture into the dialect of the Lake Macquarie natives. Whilst these laudable ends were being secured, the people themselves, however, were rapidly disappearing; and in reviewing the circumstances of his self-denying career, the devoted agent thus records the occasion of the termination of his mission: "It is a melancholy fact, that although much has been done in the way of translation, there are now scarcely any Aborigines left to learn to read, and the few who remain appear determined to go on in the broad road to destruction."[14]

Threlkeld published some of his translations and a Grammar, but as the dialects differed from district to district this was not particularly helpful to missionaries in other areas. When noting the disadvantage caused by the variety of Aboriginal dialects, Governor Darling added:

164 Besides it does not appear that any advantage has been gained by the Natives acquiring our language, which many of them speak with singular fluency and correctness. Some of these to whom I have spoken, were brought up at the School established by the late Governor Macquarie, and learned not only to read but to write. They returned however to their Tribes as soon as their Education was finished, and have remained with them in the Woods. . . .[15]

---

[13] Report from the Select Committee on the Aborigines Question, *N.S.W.L.C.V.P.*, 1838, p. 19.
[14] James Dredge, *Brief Notices on the Aborigines of New South Wales* . . ., Geelong, 1845, p. 19.
[15] Darling to Huskisson, 27 March 1828, *H.R.A.*, I, xiv, p. 55.

The Church Missionary Society at Wellington Valley

While Threlkeld was still at work at Reid's Mistake, the Church Missionary Society began a mission at Wellington Valley in 1832, first with the Rev. W. Watson and the Rev. J. S. C. Handt and, when Handt was transferred to Moreton Bay, with Watson and the Rev. James Günther. This mission lasted a little over a decade.

The first course embarked upon by all these Missionaries was to teach the natives (or at least their children) to read, as this was considered vital, that they might be able to read the Scriptures for themselves. Most of the Missionaries sought to acquire something of the native language, to assist them in conveying the message of Christianity. The C.M.S. Missionaries at Wellington Valley were no exception.

165 The Missionaries appear to have acquired a pretty competent knowledge of the Aboriginal tongue which in the neighbourhood of Wellington differs materially from the language spoken about Port Macquarie; they are also teaching two Girls and three Boys to read both in the English and Native tongues. Occasionally a number of the Blacks assist for short periods in the agricultural and horticultural operations of the Establishment and a few make themselves useful in other ways. None yet appear to have come under the influence of the Gospel; and the generality of them exhibit great repugnance to any thoughts about a future state.[16]

But as their pupils were not compelled to attend school the Missionaries sometimes had discipline problems of a kind they would not have experienced with white children.

166 When instructing the Boys, one of them refused to write, because each of those, who came yesterday, had received a new slate. I would not, at first, appear to take any particular notice of his behaviour; but when he prevented another Boy from writing by taking away his slate, I took it from him again. This made him so angry, that he threw away his pencil, and said he would go into the bush. Under such circumstances it is difficult to know how to act towards them; for if we were to punish them they would probably go away, and not return any more, and if they be not corrected at all, they become more and more careless and insolent. In this instance I told the Boy, if he did not behave better, he might as well go into the bush. But as I saw he was in no great earnest about going, I told him to look for the pencil, which he had thrown away;

---

[16] Report from Backhouse and Walker to C.M.S., 5 November 1835, C.M.S. microfilmed archives relating to the Australian and New Zealand Mission 1808–84, London, 1959.

this he did, though I did not expect it, and behaved for the present somewhat better.[17]

Occasionally the men at Wellington Valley were able to record moments of success:

167 ... Our children respond very well at Church: I am sometimes almost ready to imagine myself at St. Mary's Islington, when I hear them. They are very fond of singing; indeed, all the Natives are much attracted by music: they are almost ready to dance at the sound of the flute.[18]

The keeping of the Sabbath according to English Protestant standards was very important to the Missionaries, as the two following extracts from Handt's Journal show.

168 Three of the Blacks, who are encamped a distance from our dwelling had been fishing today. It is not easy to make them sensible of their doing wrong in breaking the Sabbath; and they will not be convinced at present that the keeping holy of the Sabbath is a duty incumbant on them.[19]

Mrs Handt had asked the boys to wash and put on shirts for Church, but they had refused and gone off into the bush.

169 In the afternoon I saw them in the camp roasting an Oppossum; thus they had been amusing themselves in hunting, preferring that employment to going to Church in comfortable clothing.[20]

Sometimes there were signs that the Aborigines were on the way to understanding the evangelical idea of the Sabbath.

170 Mrs. Watson asked Booby, the sick youth, why his hair had not been cut. He said, "Cut it to-morrow. No, not to-morrow, I believe; another day: to-morrow Sunday." It was pleasing to find that he remembered the Lord's Day, and felt that it was wrong to have his hair cut on that sacred day.[21]

William Watson was at all times anxious to gain as many Aboriginal children as he could, sometimes with complete disregard for the parents' feelings.

171 We were visited today by a Black Native, his wife and a young child at the breast. I asked them to give me the child, the

---

[17] Handt's Journal, 8 October 1834, *ibid.*
[18] Watson's Journal, C.M.S. Missionary Register for 1834, p. 508.
[19] Handt's Journal, Easter Day 1835, C.M.S. microfilmed archives.
[20] Handt's Journal, 26 April 1835, *ibid.*
[21] Watson's Journal, C.M.S. Missionary Register for 1834, p. 507.

woman seemed to feel all the mother kindling up in her bosom at the question, and clasping the infant to her breast "Bayal Bayal (no no) why me give Pickininny?"[22]

> While Watson was preoccupied with gathering the children to the mission, Günther felt it better to learn the language first.

172 I am certain it would have more contributed to the real and final success of the Mission, than that over anxiety to get the Native children before the full confidence of the Natives is obtained. Had the latter first been done the former would thus by this time be probably more easy to be effected, whilst it now seems out of question to obtain any more Native Children by consent of their parents. That you may understand more fully my argument & the justice of my remarks, I am sorry to be obliged to inform you, that as far as I have come, being upwards of 60 miles along the Macquarie and in some side way direction the Natives dread Mr. Watson on account of having taken children by force, and I being his Fellow Labourer was always in the first instance looked upon with suspicion except by such Natives who knew more about me. In various places even among the farthest Tribes they concealed their children from me. Could anything be more distressing and discouraging?[23]

> Handt complained that the colonists were hostile to missions to the Aborigines, and sought to undermine them.

173 Some of the Inhabitants of this Colony do not favour the undertaking of our Mission; and they are not backward in expressing their uncharitable sentiments in the News Paper. The chief source of their resentment is, that the money for the Mission is to be drawn from the Colonial treasury. They are endeavouring to represent the commencing of a Mission among the Aborigines of this Country to be a useless undertaking. And as they cannot defeat it in that way, they make it an object of ridicule. These unpleasant circumstances will, I hope, teach us to put our whole trust in the Lord. His Excellency, the Governor Bourke is favourable to our Missionary work. The Revd. Richard Hill performs every morning family worship in the Governor's house.[24]

> The reports of the visiting missionaries James Backhouse and George Walker to the Church Missionary Society in 1835, bore out Handt's complaints against hostile whites.

174 The State of the Mission engaged our serious attention and we felt much for the Missionaries and their wives who are employed

---

[22] Watson's Journal, 29 August 1832, C.M.S. microfilmed archives.
[23] Günther to Cowper, 8 February 1840, *ibid*.
[24] Handt to C.M.S. London, 30 July 1832, *ibid*.

in it: they have many discouragements to contend with, arising from the wandering habits of the Blacks and the demoralizing influence of Stock-keepers residing at out stations with whom the Aborigines come in contact, added to their own natural depravity which is truly appalling.

The Missionaries exert themselves to counteract these evils, but the Stock-keepers often succeed in prejudicing the minds of many of the Blacks against them so that were it not for the inducement held out to Natives in supplying them with food and blankets there is reason to believe few of them would resort to Wellington.[25]

> Backhouse and Walker identified one major problem when they saw that the Aborigines could relate more readily to the Stock-keepers than they could to the missionaries.

175 From the difference betwixt the habits of White people and those of the Blacks, there is that kind of distance between them and the Missionaries (notwithstanding much that is kind and conciliatory on the part of the latter) that appears to retard the progress of civilization and it is to be feared renders the reception of the Gospel less hopeful than it otherwise might be. Were the Missionaries to be furnished with clothing for the Blacks more like that in use among Europeans, this might in some measure be obviated, but it will be doubtful whether it will ever be overcome, until persons are raised up and prepared by the power of the Divine Grace to submit to follow these untutored people in all their wanderings and to associate with them in as familiar a manner as is compatible with moral and religious principle. A nearer assimilation to the habits of the Aboriginals— treating them in short, more as equals, is the probable cause to which may be traced the influence Stock-keepers often possess over them, [and?] it is to be apprehended generally superior to that of the Missionaries themselves. At the same time, it must be admitted that the vicious habits common to both Stock-keepers and Aborigines may often tend to increase the feelings of equality. Yet this feeling is congenial to the mind of man even in his uncivilized state, and the Missionary will do well to regard it as the exhibition of a principle deeply implanted in human nature and to shape his conduct accordingly, as much as possible descending to the level of his desired converts whenever he can do so with Christian propriety.[26]

> Nor was the behaviour of Europeans living in the vicinity of the mission station calculated to encourage the missionaries. Publicans were pro-

---

[25] Backhouse and Walker to Hill, 5 November 1835, *ibid*.
[26] *Ibid*.

hibited from selling alcohol to Aborigines, but the natives could invariably find whites who would willingly buy it for them.

176 It is lamentable to observe how soon the majority of these unfortunate Blacks fall in with European vices (of which they certainly see far more, than of good morals). Drunkenness now, since we have two public Houses in the neighbourhood, has become very general among them; they usually spend their earnings in spirituous liquors. On this account, their anxiety for money has become very great; they will hardly do any thing of consequence now without payment in money.[27]

> Günther was afraid that he was guilty of encouraging the Aborigines because he paid them in cash for washing and shearing the mission station sheep.
> The Whites outside the mission were also a negative force, in that the Aborigines did not fail to notice the difference between their conversations and those of the missionaries:

177 ... When speaking to the Natives this evening on the subject of Religion, one of them asked, "What for you speak much about God, and devil, and dying? No other white fellow, no other master, talk that way?"—It seems strange to them, and well it may, that we should always be speaking to them on those subjects which persons, even of respectability, never mention in their hearing.[28]

> Europeans also took advantage of the training given to the natives by the missionaries.

178 Many quick and promising boys have been enticed away from the Mission House by European Servants in the neighbourhood; and when it is remembered that elsewhere they are under no moral restraint, but rather encouraged in all kinds of vices, instead of its being a matter of surprise, that so few remain at the Mission House, where they are necessarily subject to controul and under discipline, it is rather remarkable that any will remain where every thing is so uncongenial with their habits and dispositions.[29]

> When the Rev. James Günther first arrived in New South Wales in 1837 to work among the Aborigines at Wellington Valley, his wife received a letter of welcome from an old friend already resident in the colony. Her words were not encouraging.

179 I am afraid Mr. Gunther will find that he has a very arduous and painful duty, for the Blacks appear to me to be in the lowest

---
[27] Günther to Colonial Secretary, 9 January 1843, *H.R.A.*, I, xxii, p. 646.
[28] Watson's Journal, C.M.S. Register for 1835, p. 518.
[29] Günther to C.M.S., in C.M.S. Register for 1846, p. 428.

grade of human creatures not even having any superstition which I thought was common to all savages, they laugh at religion, they are I think a most revolting race and as far as human appearances go to attempt civilising them appears a most unpromising task, that I most ardently wish you all success and I hope you will let me know how you get on.[30]

In fact, Günther was pleasantly surprised with his first contacts at Wellington Valley.

180 In catechising the Children today I was much pleased and surprised at the progress they have made, not only in reading the English, but also in Scriptural knowledge. Some of them would put many European children to shame. However degraded they may be, they afford at least a decisive proof, that they are quite as capable of cultivation of the mind as other nations. I feel therefore encouraged in spite of the despairing hope entertained by almost all Europeans in the Colony as it regards the civilizing and evangelizing of the poor Aborigines of this country.[31]

The missionaries certainly used every possible means to educate the Aboriginal children. They sent for the necessary apparatus to teach by what was known as the 'Infant-School System', and obviously used it with great success.

181 And surely never were human means better adapted to the design, than the Infant System is adapted to teach the Aborigines of New Holland! The pleasing and amusing manner in which instruction is presented to them, makes it rather desirable th n a task. The clapping of hands, marching &c., falls in so much with their native habits of corrobborring (dancing) that the Black children are quite delighted with it.[32]

Their work must have proved rewarding for a few years later the missionaries were able to report:

182 It is a circumstance as pleasing as it is remarkable, that all the children taught to read at the Mission House are much attached to books, consider it a severe punishment to be deprived of them, and prefer the present of a new one to almost any thing else. While they are learning the Alphabet, and to spell, they feel no interest, and the work of instruction is tedious to both the teacher and the pupil; but when they have overcome these preliminary difficulties, and are able to read so as to understand, their attention

[30] Louisa Mary Clark to Mrs. Günther, 20 May 1837, in James Günther, Correspondence 1826–78, MS. no. A1450, M.L.
[31] Günther's Journal, 8 August 1837, C.M.S. microfilmed archives.
[32] Watson's Journal, 6 December 1832, in C.M.S. Register for 1834, p. 119.

becomes excited; they begin to feel a pleasure in the employment, and never appear to be wearied with it. The Aboriginal Natives are indeed capable of attaining to the knowledge of any thing in which they may be instructed.[33]

> Nevertheless, in spite of occasional triumphs, the picture that emerged from the years of effort was one of persistent frustration. The missionaries were reluctant to baptise the Aborigines because they did not give sufficient evidence of contrition for their evil ways. Though there were times when the missionaries felt that they were making an impression, these times were few.

183 We are very apt to think our giving instruction to them is like writing on the sand, the impression of which may be effaced by the first breeze or wave that passes over it; but as we know not what thoughts are entertained by them, or how often what we have said comes into their minds, and having the promise of God, we feel it to be our duty and desire to continue to sow.[34]

> More often than not when writing their journals the missionaries could record nothing encouraging. The following is a typical entry.

184 I have nothing of any interest to relate in my journal at the present. There are very few Natives about and our occasional visits to those few, afford little worth communicating; there is so much sameness in the daily occurrences.[35]

> One of the tasks performed by the missionaries was that of administering to the sick, often a most unpleasant duty.

185 It is impossible for our friends, who are surrounded with all the comforts of civilized society, to form any thing like an adequate idea of the drudgery attendant on the Mission. I often think that a residence in a charnel-house would scarcely be more disgusting than our employment here. We have generally some sick; and occasionally from six to twelve, at the same time, destined, apparently, to an early death; filthy and corrupt in their bodies, from the ravages of disease; covered with sores; and unwilling to move from their place on any account, or to do anything for themselves: I must wash and dress their wounds, and their victuals must be prepared for and taken to them.

. . .

We have erected a small weather-boarded hut, and thatched it with reeds, for the reception of sick Natives; for we generally have

---
[33] *Ibid.*, 1839, p. 386.
[34] *Ibid.*, 1834, p. 511.
[35] Günther's Journal, 22 September 1837, C.M.S. microfilmed archives.

some here, and their loathsome condition, and dirty habits, render them unfit to reside with decent persons.[36]

In May 1840 the Corresponding Committee of the Church Missionary Society in Sydney made a request to the Governor for further aid for the mission, but the results to that date were not considered sufficient to justify any increase in the grant. The Colonial Secretary replied to the Committee in the following terms:

186   I am directed to inform you that the Governor is not aware of any engagement under which additional aid can be claimed from Government. The only ground on which such claim can be put forth must, I am to state, be a promise, or rather expectation held out by the Home Government some years ago, that in the event of success attending the Mission, further aid might be intended to it; but His Excellency laments to say that the result of a recent examination before the Executive Council, in the course of which you were yourself examined, was to prove that no success at all, or at least no success at all commensurate with the expenditure already incurred, had attended the Institution. His Excellency further desires me to state that the result of the examination has been reported, by him to the Secretary of State, and that he has been reluctantly forced to say that he cannot in the present state of the Mission recommend any increase in the annual sum allowed at present even if that sum be not discontinued. In conclusion, the Governor directs me to remark, that in the cases of other missions to the Aborigines, one half of the expenses only is supplied by Government, the rest being raised by voluntary subscriptions.[37]

The picture became gloomier with the years. Writing to his mother-in-law in 1842, Günther said:

187   I feel almost repugnant to utter again and again nothing but complaints respecting our Mission and our situation and yet I have little else to say. Trouble comes upon trouble discouragement upon discouragement disappointment upon disappointment and our prospects seem as dark as ever. The number of Natives staying with us has for a long time been very small indeed . . . the few who stayed with us have afforded very little encouragement, the best of them admit of very little to be said in their favour.[38]

After a series of quarrels, William Watson set up a separate mission nearby, taking most of the children with him. The Agricultural Assistant,

---

[36] Watson's Journal, in C.M.S. Register for 1834, pp. 503, 506.
[37] Thomson to Cowper, 19 June 1840, C.M.S. microfilmed archives.
[38] James Günther, 25 June 1842, Correspondence 1826-7, MS. no. A1450, M.L.

William Porter, was dismissed for unseemly conduct. Left alone at Wellington Valley, Günther wrote to a friend, apologizing for his delay in writing. He explained that his days were very busy, but not in a way he would have liked.

188 I wish I could say my hands have been fully occupied in Missionary pursuits. I wish I could inform you that our Blacks were so anxious and pressing for instruction that they never leave one any rest. But alas! I can say no such thing. We have long spent (I had almost said wasted) our time in endeavouring to induce them to value and seek for instruction and to get them into more decent and orderly habits whilst we have had the most harrassing life imaginable with attempting to do something we seem in reality to have done nothing or at least very little.[39]

When Günther wrote his final report to the Colonial Government in 1843 it reflected nothing of the optimism he had voiced on his arrival at Wellington Valley.

189 In attempting to furnish the Colonial Government with a Report of the State and proceedings of this Mission during the past year, I candidly acknowledge I am at a loss what to say; I would rather keep silence altogether, for I can really speak of no improvement of any consequence, either in the generality of the Aborigines of this District, or in those who are more or less attached to the Mission, whilst every year seems to bring fresh trials to add to those baneful influences, which have long acted so unfavourably upon the morals of these untutored children of the forest.[40]

Inevitably the Wellington Valley Mission closed down, and Günther reluctantly accepted the Bishop's offer of a living at Mudgee.

Other Attempts

Other missions using similar methods to those of the Anglicans fared little better. The Wesleyans at Port Phillip, like the Anglicans, concentrated on the children. Bishop Broughton reported on this mission.

190 During my residence at Port Phillip I paid a visit to the Aboriginal Institution under the superintendence of Mr. Langhorne. Some of the boys appear to be acquiring some knowledge of the art of reading, and of the most elementary truths of Religion, which it may be hoped will lead to their future improvement; but there are no apparent signs, as yet, of any impression having been made upon

---

[39] Günther to Rev. Richard Taylor, 12 November 1842, *ibid*.
[40] Günther to Colonial Secretary 9 January 1843, *H.R.A.*, I, xxii, pp. 644–5.

the adult Natives, many of whom attach themselves to the place, and derive a scanty advantage from stores or provisions which are distributed; but they have in no respect broken off their Native usages.[41]

> This mission ended in much the same way as that at Wellington Valley. The spread of settlement, the disappearance of the natives, and diseases, all played a part in the breakdown of the Wesleyans' attempt.

191 The Wesleyan Mission has failed. After laboring for ten years to inculcate the truth and lessons of Christianity upon the tribes within their reach, and to induce application to the arts of civilization, under circumstances of far greater promise seemingly than those which attended the formation and conduct of the several Government establishments, it is admitted that not a single individual has been either christianized, or civilized, and the Mission is now on the point of final abandonment.

The Aboriginal School is still carried on; at such times as the attendance of any of the Native children can be secured; but under such circumstances of discouragement, and with the appearance of so little real fruit for past exertions, that it is not hazardous to predict its ultimate failure also.[42]

> The size of the Lutheran mission at Moreton Bay, and the thought that went into its planning was seen by one Colonial newspaper as promising of success.

192 As a specimen of the spirit of devotedness to their work with which the German Missionaries have hitherto carried on their Missionary operations, it may be remarked that the Rev. K. W. Schmidt, a regularly ordained clergyman of the Prussian Church, who had studied at the Universities of Halle and Berlin, wrought like a common mechanic at the building of his own cottage at the Missionary settlement at Moreton Bay, and it is the general desire of the Missionaries to reduce the expenditure by their own labour, as much as possible [in order to afford more Missionaries].... Major Cotton, the Commandant of Moreton Bay, has expressed himself in the highest terms respecting the German Missionaries, and the single fact, that at the past and present rate of expenditure, the whole establishment of twenty adult Missionaries will have been brought out from the heart of Germany, across the vast oceans

---

[41] Bishop Broughton's statement to Diocesan Committee, 16 July 1838, in W. W. Burton, *The State of Religion and Education in New South Wales*, London, 1840, p. 242.
[42] Evidence of Superintendent of Port Phillip, 18 November 1848, Report from the Select Committee on the Aborigines and Protectorate, *N.S.W.L.C.V.P.*, 1849.

that intervene between us and that distant land, and settled and supported for two years in this colony, at the distance of not less than four hundred miles from the capital, for considerably less than it cost a single Missionary and his family, to proceed from Sydney, to his settlement in the vicinity, and to subsist for a similar period at that settlement, is proof positive of the prudence and discretion with which the whole affairs of the German Mission have been conducted. We trust, therefore, it will not fail to meet with the support it deserves.[43]

> In fact the size of the venture was one of the contributing factors towards its failure. The missionaries were so busy building homes and growing sufficient food for themselves and their families that they had little to spare for the Aborigines, and food was the chief means of drawing the Aborigines to the mission.
> A Roman Catholic mission was established on Stradbroke Island in Moreton Bay, and run by four Passionist Fathers from Italy and Switzerland. Much of the difficulty they experienced lay in the fact that they were directed from Rome, but looked for help to Archbishop Polding in Sydney, who was not a Passionist.
> In spite of their high hopes, their devotion to the Aborigines and lack of families to distract their attention, the Passionists were no more successful than any other missionaries.

193   I shall now lay before you the spiritual condition of those who have been confided to our care. Speaking for myself I am free from anxiety and very hopeful for the conversion of these Aborigines. My companions give good example by their faithful attention to everything that appertains to their own sanctification, bearing joyfully the privations that occur and availing themselves of every opportunity to learn the native language. The Aborigines can now understand us when we speak to them on the ordinary matters of everyday life. But it will take a long time and constant application before we shall be able to speak the language well, for the Aborigines are naturally inconstant and given to laziness, and they frequently leave us and wander from tribe to tribe for several days and even for a month. Indeed, it is at present two months since we have had an opportunity of conversing with them, for they set off with their wives and children for other islands, and I may say with truth, that in the seven months we have been here the Aborigines have not been with us for more than two months and a half. On one occasion, when they were going to a great distance, I ventured to accompany them, but I saw that they were not pleased. At the same time they hold us in veneration and they show us great

---

[43] *Colonist*, 2 January 1839.

affection, this being quite the reverse of the treatment of other Europeans, for these, they say, do not act kindly towards them, but betray them and deceive them, so that they have lost all confidence in them. During the whole of our residence here they have not shown by a single word or act that they dislike us. On the contrary, they give us tokens of their delight when we tell them that we shall remain always with them, and the same friendly spirit is shown by the Aborigines of Amity and Moreton, who altogether number 106. I am confident that all these will be Christians, but not till after three or four years, unless they receive very special grace and mercy from God, because it is not only difficult to remove the prejudices rooted in their minds, but as far as I can understand, they look for practical and material arguments, which alone can convince them. For that reason our work will need a long time with a great deal of patience and, above all, constant prayer for their conversion. These poor Aborigines have naturally strong passions and depraved inclinations, which require time and patience and prayer to overcome them. Among these evil dispositions of the Aborigines I may mention an extreme sloth and laziness in everything, a habit of fickleness and double-dealing, and uncontrollable vindictiveness, so much so that they will stop at nothing in the pursuit of revenge. They are deceitful and cunning and prone to lying. They are given to extreme gluttony and if possible will sleep both day and night. I say this only of the three tribes we are acquainted with. As to the Aborigines of the other islands, ours declare that they are scoundrels whom you must be on your guard against, and if they come into the neighbourhood ours at once arm themselves and make a display of the weapons we ourselves have brought. I have thus laid the true state of things before you, and it only remains for me to ask your frequent prayers that these poor Aborigines may be brought to the knowledge of the truth.[44]

The missionaries left Stradbroke Island in 1846 after a series of disappointments, food shortages and lack of assistance from Sydney. Being foreigners, they were left in a particularly difficult situation.

194 Prostrate at the feet of your Eminence I humbly and earnestly request you to obtain sufficient monetary assistance to enable me to return to Italy where, without doubt I can do a little more for my own spiritual welfare and that of my neighbour than I can do on this Mission. An unhappy experience covering five years

---

[44] Father Raymond Vaccari to Archbishop Polding, 19 December 1843, in O. Thorpe, *First Catholic Mission to the Aborigines*, Sydney, 1950, pp. 213–14.

has convinced me of this, for those years have produced nothing but useless sufferings and inconveniences.[45]

> One of the Fathers settled in South Australia, the others dispersed to various parts of the world. Cardinal Moran quoted a revealing statement made by one who revisited the mission some years after its abandonment.

195   A few further details are supplied by the Venerable Monsignor Archdeacon Rigney, who is still living and who entered on the spiritual charge of the Brisbane district as far back as the year 1858. "The missionaries left the station at Stradbroke Island, in 1846, and twelve years afterwards the writer of these lines visited the place in company with an old servant of the Fathers—Peter Hartley. The buildings were in ruins, the island was deserted, and only one black was met with in the bay. He was a young man of twenty-four or twenty-five years. He had learnt to serve Mass when a boy, but all traces of his religious education had completely vanished from his mind. He could not make the sign of the cross nor understand what was done when others made it, and not one word of the Lord's Prayer could he say, although Peter Hartley—who knew him well and saw him often serving Mass—tried to bring back former lessons to his mind."[46]

> By the end of 1842 it was clear that the efforts of the missionaries had failed or were doomed to failure. The Mission at Wellington Valley was folding up, the Passionists at Stradbroke Island were making little headway, and the Wesleyans at Port Phillip were beginning to feel the hopelessness of their task. Lord Stanley was reluctant to believe that the failure of the Missions marked the failure of attempts to 'civilize' the Aborigines.

196   I have the honor to acknowledge the receipt of your Despatches . . ., reporting the information which has reached you, in respect to the Aboriginal Tribes of New South Wales, and the result of the attempts which have been made, under the sanction of Her Majesty's Government, to civilize and protect these people.

I have read with great attention, but with deep regret, the accounts contained in these Despatches, after making every fair allowance for the peculiar difficulty of such an undertaking; it seems impossible any longer to deny that the efforts, which have hitherto been made for the civilization of the Aborigines, have been unavailing; that no real progress has yet been effected; and that there is no reasonable ground to expect from them greater success in future.

---

[45] Father Maurice Lencioni to the Cardinal Prefect of the Sacred Congregation of the Propaganda, 1 May 1848, *ibid.*, p. 221.
[46] Cardinal Moran, *History of the Catholic Church in Australasia*, Sydney [1900?], p. 419.

You will be sensible with how much pain and reluctance I have come to this opinion; but I cannot shut my eyes to the conclusion which inevitably follows from the Statements which you have submitted to me on the subject.

Your Despatch of the 11th March last, No. 50, contains an account of the several Missions up to that date, with reports likewise from the Chief Protector and his Assistants, and from the Crown Land Commissioners. The Statements respecting the Missions, furnished not by their opponents nor even by indifferent parties, but by the Missionaries themselves, are I am sorry to say as discouraging as it is possible to be. In respect to the Mission at Wellington Valley, Mr. Günther writes in a tone of despondency, which shows that he has abandoned the hope of success. The opening of his Report is indeed a plain admission of despair, I sincerely wish that his facts did not bear out such a feeling. But when he reports that, after a trial of ten years, only one of all, who have been attached to the Mission, "affords some satisfaction and encouragement"; that of the others, only four still remain with them, and that these continually absent themselves, and when at home evince but little desire for instruction; that "their thoughtlessness, a spirit of independence, ingratitude, and want of sincere straightforward dealing, often try us in the extreme"; That drunkenness is increasing; and that the Natives are "gradually swept away by debauchery and other evils, arising from their intermixture with Europeans".

I acknowledge that he has stated enough to warrant his despondency, and to show that it proceeds from no momentary disappointment alone, but from a settled and reasonable Conviction.

Nor do the other Missions hold out any greater encouragement. That at Moreton Bay is admitted by Mr. Handt to have made but little progress, as neither children nor adults can be persuaded to stay for any length of time; while that at Lake McQuarrie had, at the date of your Despatch, ceased to exist from the extinction or removal of the Natives formerly in its vicinity. The Wesleyan Missionaries at Port Philip, notwithstanding an expenditure in 1841 of nearly £1,300, acknowledge that they are "far from being satisfied with the degree of success which has attended our Labours", and "that a feeling of despair sometimes takes possession of our minds and weighs down our spirits", arising from the frightful mortality among the Natives.

In the face of such representations, which can be attributed neither to prejudice nor misinformation, I have great doubts as to the wisdom or propriety of continuing the Missions any longer. I fear that to do so would be to delude ourselves with the mere idea of doing something, which would be injurious to the Natives as interfering with other and more advantageous arrangements, and unjust to the Colony, as continuing an unnecessary and profitless expenditure.

To this conclusion, I have been led by your Despatch No. 50; but, anticipating that the Protectorate System would promise more beneficial results, I postpone my instructions in the matter until I should receive some further information.[47]

The Protectorate System will be dealt with in the following chapter.

[47] Stanley to Gipps, 20 December 1842, *H.R.A.*, I, xxii, pp. 436–7.

7
The Protectorate

It was clear that the missionaries were not reaping rewards commensurate with their great efforts and vast expenditure. They had neither converted the Aborigines to Christianity nor encouraged more than a few of them to adopt white man's civilization. The land-hungry settlers resented the large land-grants made to the missions, and the wretched Aborigines were made still more wretched as Europeans advanced over their tribal lands.

Humanitarians in England, concerned not only with the Aborigines of Australia, but with native peoples throughout the British Empire, succeeded in having appointed, in 1835, a Select Committee of the House of Commons to enquire into the condition of Aborigines in British settlements. The Rev. Dr J. D. Lang submitted to the Committee written evidence, in which he outlined a scheme for the use of Protectors to work among the Aborigines of Australia:

197   The first duty of the Government . . ., considered as acting in the capacity of trustee for the aborigines, is to protect them from aggression; and this duty, I conceive, could be discharged most effectually by appointing a suitable person as Protector of the aborigines, to act under the direction and control of a Board of Protection, to consist of certain officers of the Government, certain ministers of religion of various denominations, and certain private gentlemen in the colony, distinguished for their active philanthropy.

The office of Protector of the Aborigines would be best filled by a young man of intelligence and activity, of Christian principles, of unshrinking firmness and mild demeanor. The salary would not require to be above 150 *l.* per annum, with an allowance for travelling expenses; and the source from which the whole cost of the office would be legitimately defrayed, would be the revenue arising from the sale of land. The duties of the Protector of the Aborigines would be, to enquire into the circumstances and condition of the black natives throughout the territory, by visiting each district at stated times, agreeably to the direction of the Board; to investigate every case of injury or aggression on the aborigines that might come to his knowledge, and to bring the offender to justice, either in a court of law, or by detailing the case in one or other of the public journals of the colony; and to act in all other particulars for their general benefit, agreeably to the instructions of the board.

The Board of Protection should meet quarterly, monthly or weekly, as circumstances might render expedient. Their duties should be to take into consideration the state of the aborigines generally, and to devise ways and means of carrying into effect the beneficent intentions of His Majesty's Government in their behalf; to undertake the superintendence of all measures and operations undertaken for securing their comfortable subsistence, their civilization, their general education, and their christianization.

The second duty of the Government towards the Aborigines is, to secure to them such a measure of comfortable subsistence as their migratory habits, and their obstinate rejection of the habits of civilization, would enable them to attain. This duty would be most effectually discharged under the direction of the Board of Protection, who should report to the Government from time to time, and make suggestions and recommendations as they should deem expedient.[1]

> In the Report issued by this Select Committee, specific suggestions were made with regard to the duties of the office of Protector.

198 The duties of the Protectors of the Aborigines in New Holland should consist, first, in cultivating a personal knowledge of the natives, and a personal intercourse with them; and with that view these officers should be expected to acquire an adequate familiarity with the native language. To facilitate the growth of confidence, the Protectors should be furnished with some means of making to the tribes occasional presents of articles either of use or ornament, of course abstaining from the gift of liquors. The Protectors should ascertain what is that species of industry which is least foreign to the habits and disposition of the objects of their care, and should be provided with all the necessary means of supplying them with such employment. Especially they should claim for the maintenance of the Aborigines such lands as may be necessary for their support. So long as agriculture shall be distasteful to them, they should be provided with the means of pursuing the chase without molestation. The education of the young will of course be amongst the foremost of the cares of the missionaries; and the Protectors should render every assistance in their power in advancing this all-important part of any general scheme of improvement.

In the event of a native being slain, it should be the duty of the

---

[1] Lang to T. F. Buxton, 10 June 1834, in evidence to Select Committee on Aborigines (British Settlements), *B.P.P.*, Vol. VII, p. 683.

Protector to perform, as far as the nature of the case will admit, the office of coroner.

To require from the ignorant hordes of savages living in Eastern or Western Australia the observance of our laws would be absurd, and to punish their non-observance of them by severe penalties would be palpably unjust. On the other hand, if they are placed beyond the pale of the law as a rule of their conduct to others, they will infallibly lose the advantage of it, considered as a rule of conduct of others towards them. To determine under what special regulations they should be placed, is a task to be performed only by those who can study the question with the aid of the most minute and close local observation. It should therefore be one branch of the duty of the Protectors to suggest to the local Government, and through it to the local Legislature, such short and simple rules as may form a temporary and provisional code for the regulation of the Aborigines, until advancing knowledge and civilization shall have superseded the necessity for any such special laws.

The practice of employing the Aborigines as a species of police to detect and counteract the thefts practised by the convicts in the remoter districts of the Colony should be prevented or discouraged by the Protectors. It is not difficult thus to enlist the instinct and passions of uncivilized men in defence of order; but they invariably become the victims of their own zeal in this service. The deadly antipathy which was excited between the Aborigines and the Bush-rangers of Van Diemen's Land provoked a series of outrages which would have terminated in the utter extermination of the whole race, if the local Government had not interposed to remove the last remnant of them from the island; an act of real mercy, though of apparent severity. The Aborigines of New Holland have enough to undergo and to fear from their contact with a convict population, without aggravating the evil by fostering a bitter personal antipathy between them.

Each Protector of Aborigines should be invested with the character of a magistrate, and should be required to promote the prosecution of all crimes committed against their persons or their property; while in the event of any of them being charged with the commission of such offences, the Protector should, either in person or through the agency of some practitioner of the law, to be employed and instructed by him, undertake and superintend the defence of the accused party.

Finally, the Protector should be required to make periodical reports to the local Government of all his proceedings in the execution of the duties of his office, with every suggestion which increasing experience might enable him to offer for advancing the interests and maintaining the security of the objects of his care. The local Government should, in its turn, be required to transmit those reports to this kingdom, with a report of the proceedings taken or contemplated in furtherance of the recommendations of the Protector. The collection of accurate statistical information should be one of the principal objects of these periodical reports. It is probable that the depopulation and decay of many tribes which, in different parts of the world, have sunk under European encroachments, would have been arrested in its course, if the progress of the calamity had from time to time been brought distinctly under the notice of any authority competent to redress the wrong. In many cases, the first distinct apprehension of the reality and magnitude of the evil has not been acquired until it was ascertained that some uncivilized nation had ceased to exist.[2]

> As a result of the Select Committee's recommendations, Lord Glenelg sent the following instructions to Sir George Gipps, Governor of New South Wales:

199   In transmitting to you a Duplicate copy of the last Report of the Select Committee of the House of Commons on Aborigines, I have the honor to communicate to you that H.M. Govt. have directed their anxious attention to the adoption of some plan for the better protection and civilisation of the Native Tribes within the limits of your Government.

With that view, it has been resolved to appoint at once a small number of persons qualified to fill the office of Protector of Aborigines. I have confined that number in the first instance to one Chief Protector, aided by four Assistant Protectors. I would propose that the Chief Protector should fix his principal station at Port Philip, as the most convenient point from whence he could traverse the surrounding country and be in personal communication with his Assistants; two of whom should occupy the country to the Northward and Eastward, and the other two be stationed to the Northward and as far Westward as the Boundaries of the Colony of South Australia.

I propose to confer the Office of Chief Protector on Mr. Robinson, who, you are no doubt aware, has for some time past been in charge of the Aboriginal Establishment at Flinders Island, and who has shewn himself to be eminently qualified for such an Office. I shall direct the Lt. Governor of V.D. Land to communicate my intentions to Mr. Robinson and to take the necessary measures for sending him to Sydney, if he should be prepared to undertake the Office.

. . .

---

[2] Report from Select Committee on Aborigines (British Settlements), *ibid.*, pp. 83–4.

With regard to the expences attending the Establishment, it is proposed to assign to the Chief Protector a Salary of £500 per Annum, and to each of the Assistants £250. The four officers proceeding from this Country will also have an allowance of £100 each on account of their outfit and Passage, and, according to the General rule of this Department, they have been informed that they will receive Half Salary from the date of Embarkation.

It will be necessary to make some provision to enable the Protectors to supply the natives occasionally with moderate quantities of Food and Clothing.

In fixing this Expenditure, H.M. Govt. have anticipated the Concurrence of the Legislative Council of your Government in voting the necessary Sum for meeting the Charge. The object contemplated is so important, and the obligation, which rests on the Colonists to do their utmost for the protection and civilization of the Native Tribes, so imperative, that I am convinced no further argument is necessary to induce a cheerful co-operation on their part in the measure now adopted. If the Aboriginal Establishment at Flinders Island should be broken up and transferred to New South Wales, some portion of the Expenditure might reasonably be defrayed from the Revenues of V.D. Land.

It remains for me to explain my general view of the duties, which will devolve on the Protectors, and to refer to the points which will form the ground of Instructions which you will issue to them.

1. Each Protector should attach himself as closely and constantly as possible to the Aboriginal Tribes, who may be found in the District for which he may be appointed; attending them, if practicable, in their movements from one place to another, until they can be induced to assume more settled habits of life; and endeavouring to conciliate their respect and confidence, and to make them feel that he is their friend.

2. He must watch over the rights and interests of the Natives, protect them, as far as his personal exertions and influence, from any encroachment on their property, and from acts of Cruelty, of oppression or injustice and faithfully represent their wants, wishes or grievances, if such representation be found necessary, thro' the Chief Protector, to the Government of the Colony. For this purpose, it will be desirable to invest each Protector with a Commission as Magistrate.

3. If the Natives can be induced in any considerable numbers to locate themselves in a particular place, it will be the object of the Protector to teach and encourage them to engage in the cultivation of the grounds, in building suitable Habitations for themselves, and in whatever else may conduce to their civilization and social improvement.

4. The Education and Instruction of the Children, as early and as extensively as it may be practicable, is to be regarded as a matter of primary importance.

5. In connection with the engagements, and as affording the most efficient means for the ultimate accomplishment of them, the Assistant Protector should promote to the utmost extent of his ability and opportunity the *moral* and *religious* improvement of the Natives, by instructing them in the Elements of the Christian Religion, and preparing them for the reception of Teachers, whose peculiar province it would be to promote the knowledge and practice of Christianity among them.

6. In reference to every object contemplated by the proposed Appointment, it is exceedingly desirable that the Protector should, as soon as possible, learn the language of the Natives so as to be able freely and familiarly to converse with them.

7. He must take charge of and be accountable for any provisions or clothing, which may be placed under his care for distribution to the Natives.

8. He will obtain as accurate information as may be practicable of the number of the natives within his District, and of all important particulars in regard to them.

These appear to me the principal points which demand attention in reference to this subject. But it is of course not my intention to restrict you in the Instructions, which you will have to issue to the Protector, within the topics on which I have touched, as your local knowledge and experience will doubtless enable you to supply omissions in the outline which I have given.[3]

> Mr Sievewright, Mr Thomas, Mr Dredge and Mr Parker were named by Glenelg as Assistant Protectors. When reporting their arrival in the Colony, Gipps raised the question of allowances, which the Protectors claimed they had been promised.

200 The four assistant Protectors, who arrived by different vessels from England, are as yet in Sydney, but they are to remove to Port Phillip as soon as a conveyance can be provided for themselves and families, and are there to await the arrival of Mr. Robinson.

Your Lordship informed me that the salary of each of these four gentlemen has been fixed at £250 per annum; but, in addition to salary, they claim various allowances and advantages, which they say were promised them in your Lordship's name by Sir George Arthur: they will evidently require some equipment to enable them

---

[3] Glenelg to Gipps, 31 January 1838, *H.R.A.*, I, xix, pp. 252-3, 254-5.

to enter upon their duties, but I am not able yet to report to your Lordship what the expence of it may be.[4]

> Early reports were fairly encouraging, although the Protectors, like the missionaries, found the whites to be a great impediment. The following extracts are taken from a very long letter written by the Chief Protector, Mr Robinson, to the Superintendent of the Port Phillip District, Charles Joseph La Trobe:

201   Four reserves have been sanctioned for the Geelong or Western District; and the central station is about to be occupied.

The homesteads of the Assistant Protectors are intended to serve as the centre of operations for their districts, and as an asylum for such Aboriginal natives as are disposed to settle. Agricultural and horticultural operations are to be carried on at those stations for the exclusive benefit and advantage of the natives. Those who are able are expected to give an equivalent for what they receive. The sick, the aged, and young children are to be rationed.

No settler is allowed to occupy land within five miles of the Assistant Protector's station. These establishments are not, in any way, to interfere with the itinerating duties of the Assistant Protectors; but on the contrary, are meant to render their services more efficient.

They are to travel among and sojourn with the native tribes, and by every possible means in their power, endeavour to induce them to a settled mode of existence.

In adverting to the fixed establishments I have thought it desirable to do so generally rather than in detail, as at this juncture it might, and with some propriety, considering the brief period of their formation, be deemed premature. Now that the establishments are formed, and the Aborigines in tolerable numbers frequent those institutions, I would respectively bring under notice the propriety that properly qualified persons, as recommended in the Right Honorable the Secretary of State's Despatch, be appointed for the purpose of imparting religious instruction, and of administering to this hapless race the blessings of christianity.

This aid is necessary, and I feel assured that the civilization of the Aborigines cannot progress unless it be conceded. The Australasian Aborigines, like all other savage nations, are superstitious, and I know of no other means so effectual for removing those prejudices, as the one submitted.

The Aborigines are capable of being instructed, and if their condition be not improved, the fault, I feel assured, if I may so speak, cannot be wholly attributable to them, for from my personal

---

[4] Gipps to Glenelg, 10 November 1838, *ibid.*, pp. 668–9.

intercourse with the tribes, I have found them in general intelligent, possessing intellect and capacity of no ordinary description, and in this respect, fully equal to a large majority of the peasantry of civilized communities. All the tribes, even the most ferocious, can be communicated with; this I assert, with confidence, having myself personally conferred with a large majority of the native inhabitants of this province. During my late expedition of five months in the western interior, I was never without natives; and on my previous expeditions to the northward, north-eastward, and north-west, was always in communication with them.

. . .

Every endeavour is made at the several establishments to induce the natives to habits of industry, and I am happy to state, that the reports of the Assistant Protectors on this head, are perfectly satisfactory. The natives in all cases, are taught to feel that their occupation is for their own advantage, and this, with untutored men, is the great incitement to industry.

The Assistant Protector at the Lodden thus writes,—"The Aborigines were employed in every description of labour that could be created, and the results, as will be indicated by subsequent statements, were very satisfactory. Since the occupation of the present station on the upper branch of the Lodden, ample employment has been furnished, in cultivating the ground, building, fencing, and other labour incident to a new station." When great bodily exertion is not requisite, the Aboriginal natives are fully equal to Europeans, but in severe labour they are inferior; they have sufficient capacity for acquiring knowledge; but a want of stability, especially with the adults, is much felt. To each central station, an overseer has been appointed to conduct the farming operations, and take charge of the stores; and it is expected ere long, that the produce raised, will be sufficient for the support of the inhabitants. Every endeavour, as far as the means at my disposal permitted, have been made to improve the moral and social condition of the Aborigines. Religious services are performed by the Sub-Protectors on the Sabbath, at the central stations, and in their absence by the overseers; persons of moral and religious character have been invariably recommended for subordinate situations; but, notwithstanding these endeavours, I do think I should ill discharge my duty to the Aborigines and to the Government, if I failed to represent the necessity that exists, for properly qualified persons being appointed to impart to this portion of the human family the blessings of christian instruction, and to superintend the scholastic duties; on the subject of encouraging natives to engage in the service of settlers, I, at present, do not think I could consistently recommend as a general principle, even were it practicable, such a measure; for although many of the settlers, to my knowledge, are kind and humane, and highly respectable, and who would be very proper persons to take an interest in the affairs of the natives, (had we a better class of peasantry) yet I do think it it would be extremely injudicious under existing circumstances to do so, for although this province has not ranked as a penal Colony, still a large proportion of the men employed, until very lately, once belonged to those classes; Van Diemen's Land, and the middle Districts supplied a large proportion, and these, for the most part, were of the worst character; of this class were the greater part of the men I met in my late and protracted journey into the western interior, and it grieved me to observe with what perfect recklessness and impunity, profane swearing was had recourse to; by them the Sabbath was not only disregarded, but desecrated, and from their animosity to the natives, (for it was too apparent to be misunderstood) it was easy to imagine the kind of treatment the natives would receive when the opportunity offered for perpetrating it. The saying was common with the settlers "that the men and not we are the masters"

If therefore the settlers could not control their men in matters where they were personally concerned, it was scarcely to be supposed they could do so in matters regarding the natives; and on that account many of the respectable settlers assured me they kept the natives from their runs, and prohibited their servants from holding any intercourse with them.[5]

It was not long before the Protectorate came under criticism. The settlers objected to the large sums of money being expended:

202 *Black Protectorate.*—This worse than useless department cost the colonists of New South Wales no less than *five thousand and fifty two pounds* last year. Truly, this is "paying too dear for our whistle", if we even derive any benefits from it. Such lavish expenditure of the public funds, at a time when the head of the colonial government is lachrymosely bewailing the low state of our finances, is irritating. His Excellency rather *piques* himself upon being a skilful financier; but, while such an egregious and palpable waste of public money is thus uselessly squandered annually, under his Excellency's immediate countenance and sanction, we cannot give him the credit he demands for his economy in the distribution of the funds. The Black Protectorate and the Commissioners of Crown Lands' Department are, we hesitate not to pronounce, amongst the most wasteful impositions that ever weighed down an infant colony struggling

---

[5] Robinson to La Trobe, 11 December 1841, *N.S.W.L.C.V.P.*, 1843, pp. 19, 20.

into maturity; and were it not for the fecundity of our internal resources of wealth we could not endure them another twelvemonth.[6]

> The complaints were not only voiced by the newspapers. One missionary reported to his London headquarters that the efforts of the Protectors, being entirely secular, and conducted for white man's self-interest, could never be wholly successful—he advocated the appointment of ministers of religion.

203 Let the Government then reserve suitable portions of land within the territorial limits of the respective tribes, forming thereon depots for supplying them with provisions and clothing under the charge of individuals of exemplary character, taking at the same time an interest in their welfare, and who would endeavour to instruct them in agriculture and other useful arts; and let there be a minister appointed to take the spiritual charge and to conduct the whole establishment on strictly Missionary principles. This is the plan which has been recently laid before His Excellency Sir George Gipps, in a Memorial which was drawn up by the Gentlemen of this District, a copy of which has been forwarded to you. In this Memorial these Gentlemen speak of the inutility of the Protectorate, and the Border Police, and advise the sole adoption of Missionary labours, as the only effectual means of civilizing the blacks, and securing peace and protection to the whites. The Protectorate and Border Police are two distinct systems which have been introduced and set in motion within the last two years and a half, for the protection of the black and white population. I think those systems, the Protectorate especially would be productive of Good if it were not cramped in its operations, and if it were conducted on a well digested, liberal, and extensive plan.[7]

> Another missionary suggested that missionaries and Protectors should work together.

204 The Protectorate under Government are doing some thing, but as things are, their efforts are comparatively feeble. Indeed all the Civil protection that can be extended to them without the Gospel will avail but little; the Missionary and the Protector cannot be combined in one individual—their duties would be in many respects adverse to each other; even if pious, self denying men could be obtained to discharge the obligations of a Protector. But civil protection alone cannot possibly save them from gradual extermination as Europeans increase in number and possession of their

---

[6] *Australian*, 4 August 1840.
[7] F. Tuckfield to Wesleyan Missionary Society, 30 September 1840, Bonwick Transcripts, Box 54, M.L.

country. It cannot save their precious souls—they will perish as a people—their never dying souls are daily perishing for lack of knowledge—and their blood will rest upon a *guilty Christian Nation*.

If anything can save them from a wretched, pining and *murderous* extinction, and their immortal souls from eternal misery, it is a Gospel provision and *protection*; which must be made without delay. I have sufficient authority to state that His Honor J. C. Latrobe, Esq. the Provincial Governor is particularly anxious that more Missionaries should be sent without delay. The Chief Protector appears to be equally so; he has called upon me repeatedly to beg me to try to prevail with our Committee to send out men, who, he promises, should receive every facility in his power. The feeling public of Australia Felix join issue in the important subject, and say that to accomplish the great objects of their spiritual and temporal amelioration Missionaries must be sent. And all seem to concur in the opinion that our Society can send out men the best adapted to the arduous work. The prevailing opinion grounded upon experience and observation is, that a Missionary must be appointed to each principal tribe, as their several languages vary so materially, and they cannot by any means be induced to intermingle.

If the Missionaries could co-operate with the Protectors without being *in anywise shackled* by such coadjutancy it might be well; as the Missionaries would be relieved from embarrassing expensive temporalities, and left to uninterrupted pursuit of their proper work.[8]

It seemed to some that the arrival of the Protectors in the Port Phillip District had marked a worsening of the relationships between black and white, and that hostilities were more serious than ever. Gipps told the Secretary of State:

205 With my Despatch of the 7th May last, No. 61, I had the honor to forward to Your Lordship a number of documents illustrative of the nature of the intercourse, which exists in this Colony between the European Settlers and the Aboriginal Inhabitants, an intercourse which is unhappily marked by acts of violence on both sides.

I have now the honor to forward further documents of the same nature, selected in like manner as before out of an immense mass of Papers, the correspondence on matters connected with the Aborigines having, since the appointment of the Protectors, increased to such a degree as to form, I lament to say, of itself no inconsiderable evil.

Your Lordship will I am sure be sorry to learn that aggressions

---

[8] J. Orton [to unknown recipient], 5 January 1841, *ibid*.

by the Natives on the flocks and herds of the Settlers, as well as the acts of reprisal to which they give birth, have during the last few months in the Port Phillip District increased rather than decreased in number.[9]

> The Governor then outlined some recent occurrences in the District which illustrated his point. From this he drew several conclusions.

206   Your Lordship will I am sure observe with regret that all the occurrences, alluded to in this Despatch, have taken place in those Districts of the Colony, for which Protectors of Aborigines were especially appointed by Her Majesty's Government, namely in the neighbourhood of Port Phillip, the older parts of the Colony having been, I rejoice to say, during the last six months but little disturbed with any outrages between Blacks and Whites.

By many of the Settlers, it is said that the presence of the Protectors is the occasion of outrage, inasmuch as their appointment has tended to embolden the Blacks, and to render the Stockmen or Servants of the Settlers less resolute than they used to be in defence of their Masters' property. I am myself far more disposed to attribute the increased frequency of collisions of this nature to the cause which I have already alluded to, namely, the rapidity with which people have been led from the superiority of its pasturage to form New Stations in the Port Phillip District, and by which a tract of country has been rapidly occupied by Europeans, which was until very recently the undisputed heritage of the Savage; at the same time however, I feel it my duty to declare that my hopes of any advantage being derived from the employment of the Protectors are every day diminishing.

The Chief Protector, whatever may be his other merits (and on the more confined theatre on which he acted in Van Diemen's Land I believe they were considerable), is afflicted with such a love of writing that much of his time must be spent in that way, which would be much better devoted to active employment; and his assistants are I believe even more inactive than he is; they are all encumbered, as I have before had occasion to observe, with large families, and seem to have come to Australia with the expectation of establishing Missionary Stations, rather than of itinerating with and amongst the tribes. One of them has already resigned, as reported in My Despatch of the 7th May last; another never quitted for more than a year the spot on which he first seated himself, called the Salt Water River, though there were no Blacks there; and the Chief Protector has himself, in a letter to Mr. La Trobe of the 22nd Septt., 1840, described it "as the worst that could possibly have been selected,

---

[9] Gipps to Russell, 3 February 1841, *H.R.A.*, I, xxi, p. 208.

being quite out of the way of communication with the Chief Tribes of the District, and thickly surrounded with Settlers".

Mr. La Trobe has complained nearly in terms as strong of the difficulty of getting another to move from Geelong.

In my Despatch of the 7th May last, I reported to Your Lordship that I had sanctioned the formation of a homestead of fixed station for each Assistant Protector with a sufficiency of land attached to it to keep Settlers at a distance.

The formation of these Stations will doubtless tend to give a still more Missionary character to the duties of the Protectors. Each homestead will in fact become the seat of an establishment, nearly similar to that of Wellington Valley; though, being more under the superintendence of the Executive Government, it is to be hoped that the causes, which have rendered the Mission at Wellington of little use, may be obviated.

The principal advantage of such Missions or Stations is that they may, under proper management, be made places of refuge to the Natives and of Education for their Children; the Education of children being perhaps the only measure, on which a reasonable hope can now be founded for effecting any improvement in the Aborigines of New South Wales.

It is evident, however, that Protectors, whose duties are confined to Missions of this sort, can exercise no influence whatever in checking the atrocities which are committed, whenever land is occupied for the first time by the flocks or herds of our Settlers. Young men, unencumbered with families, are best suited for these purposes; and accordingly I have universally selected such to be our Commissioner of Crown Lands.[10]

> A little over a year later Gipps reported to England with more evidence of the failure of the Protectorate system.

207 Connected with the subject of my Despatches of this day's date, Nos. 89 and 90, I forward herewith, a Copy of a letter, addressed to the Colonial Secretary of this Colony by Mr. La Trobe, representing to me, in a more formal manner than he had theretofore done, the inefficiency of the Department, which was organized in 1839 in the District of Port Phillip for the protection of the Aborigines.

When this letter reached me, I entertained doubts as to the necessity or propriety of forwarding it to Your Lordship; but since I have received from Mr. La Trobe the additional information, contained in the papers forwarded with my Despatches above alluded to of this day's date, I feel that I ought not to withhold it.

[10] *Ibid.*, pp. 210–11.

With the exception of the Chief Protector (Mr. Robinson), it would be difficult I think to find men less equal to the arduous duty of acting as Protectors of the Aborigines than those, who were selected for this purpose in England in the year 1838; and the Chief Protector, though efficient as far as his own mode of holding intercourse with the Blacks is concerned, is quite unequal to the control of what is becoming a large and expensive Department; and moreover he is already advanced in years and far beyond the prime of life.

The course pursued by the Protectors has been, as far as I am able to form a judgment of it, one from the beginning of feeble action and puling complaint. With power in their hands to command the respect of the Settlers, they have failed to make themselves respected; and I greatly fear that their measures have tended rather to increase than allay the irritation, which has long existed between the two Races.[11]

> Lord Stanley was clearly disappointed by the apparent collapse of the Protectorate, following, as it did, so closely upon the closure of the various missions. He was unable to believe that the Australian Aborigines were the only people in the world incapable of adopting Christianity and European civilization.

208   Your despatches of the 16th and 20th May have furnished that further information; although they contradict the hopes which I had been led to entertain after the distinct and unequivocal opinion announced by Mr. Latrobe, supported as it is by the expression of your concurrence, I cannot conceal from myself that the failure of the system of Protectors has been, at least, as complete as that of the Missions.

I have no doubt that a portion of this ill success, perhaps a large portion, is attributable to the want of sound judgment and zealous activity on the part of the assistant protectors. Thus the practice of collecting large bodies of the Natives in one spot, and in the immediate vicinity of the Settlers, without any previous provision for their subsistence or employment, was a proceeding of singular indiscretion. That these people would commit depredations rather than suffer want, and that thus ill blood and probably collisions would be caused between them and the Settlers, must, I should have thought, occurred to any man of common observation; and no one could have better reason than Mr. Sievewright to know his utter inability to controul them, when such a course could be adopted. I am not surprised at your opinion that the measures of

---

[11] Gipps to Stanley, 16 May 1842, *ibid.*, xxii, pp. 54–5.

the protectors have tended "rather to increase than allay the irritation which has long existed between the two races".

But, after allowing for the effect of such errors, and for the possibility of preventing their recurrence, there is yet enough in Mr. Latrobe's reports to shew that the system itself is defective, at least in the hands of those whose services we are able to command.

I am unwilling, at this distance from the Scene and without that minute local knowledge which is essential, to give you any precise instructions as to the course which under present circumstances should be pursued. But I have the less hesitation in leaving the matter in your hands, because your whole Correspondence shews that no one feels more strongly than yourself the duty as well as the policy of protection, and, if possible, civilizing these Aborigines, and of promoting a good understanding between them and the white Settlers; at present, though I am far from attributing to the white Settlers generally an ill disposition towards the Natives, there is an apparent want of feeling among them, where the Natives are concerned, which is much to be lamented. Outrages of the most atrocious description, involving sometimes considerable loss of life, are spoken of, as I observe in these papers, with an indifference and lightness, which to those at a distance is very shocking. I cannot but fear that the feeling which dictates this mode of speaking, may also cause the difficulty in discovering and bringing to Justice the perpetrators of the outrages, which from time to time occur.

With a view to the protection of the Natives, the most essential step is to correct the temper and tone adopted by the Settlers. Whatever may depend on your own personal influence, or on the zealous co-operation of Mr. Latrobe, will, I am sure, be done at once, and I will not doubt that your efforts in this respect will be successful. In regard to the Missions and the Protectors, I give you no definite Instructions; if, at your receipt of this Despatch, you should see no greater prospect of advantage than has hitherto appeared, you will be at liberty to discontinue the grants to either as early as possible; but, if circumstances should promise more success for the future, the grants may be continued for such time as may be necessary to bring the matter to a certain result.[12]

> Following this expression of the Secretary of State's attitude, Gipps sought to give the Protectors a longer trial, and at the same time to overcome the settlers' objections to the large sums of money spent on the Protectors and the Native Police. The following document illustrates this point, while giving a description of the work of the Native Police.

[12] Stanley to Gipps, 20 December 1842, *ibid.*, pp. 438-9.

209   Having, with my Despatch of this day's date No. 68, transmitted to Your Lordship the Annual Reports for 1843 from Officers of this Government, engaged in the protection or civilization of the Aborigines, I think the present a proper occasion to address Your Lordship generally respecting this unhappy race of People.

In so doing, I have first to acknowledge the receipt of your Lordship's Despatch, No. 225 of the 20th December, 1842, wherein the painful conclusions were communicated to me, which Your Lordship had been forced to draw from the Reports, transmitted in former years from the Heads of the different Missions in this Colony, and from the Officers of Government engaged in the protection or civilization of the Aborigines. I have not thought it right, in consequence of the receipt of that Despatch entirely to break up the Establishments of the Protectors of Aborigines in the Port Phillip District; but I have made arrangements with Mr. La Trobe to keep the expenses of them in the current year within the sum of £3,000, a degree of economy which is further rendered necessary by the diminution in the productiveness of the Crown or Territorial Revenue, and the additional charge which is thrown upon it by the refusal of the Legislative Council any longer to provide for the Department of the Surveyor General, out of the funds which are under the control of the Council. This expenditure is, however, exclusive of that which is occasioned by the maintenance of the Border Police, one half of which is usually considered to be incurred on account of the Aborigines.

It is exclusive also of the expense of a "Native Police", composed altogether of Aborigines, which I now beg leave for the first time to bring under Your Lordship's observation.

It has long been customary in this Colony to resort to the assistance of the Aborigines in tracking offenders (Bushrangers as they are commonly called); and, for some years past, I have endeavoured permanently to attach two or three Aboriginal Natives to each Party of the Border Police, as well as to the more regular Force called the "Mounted Police"; but it is only in the Port Phillip District that a Corps consisting entirely of Aboriginals has been extablished.

The first attempt at the formation of such a Corps was made in 1836 or 1837, soon after the opening of Port Phillip, under an Officer of the name of De Villiers; but it led to no satisfactory result; and the project was abandoned or rather remained in abeyance until the beginning of 1842, when Mr. La Trobe revived it, and placed at the head of the Establishment a gentleman named Dana (an Englishman), by whom the experiment has been very satisfactorily conducted.

The Establishment of the "Native Police", distinct either from the Mounted or Border Police, first appeared on the Port Phillip Estimates for the year 1843, when the sum of £2,675 5s. was voted for the support of it; and, on the estimates for the current year, the sum of £2,420 was voted by the present Council for the like purpose.

Copies of ... Papers, respecting the formation and progress of the Native Police ... strongly confirm the opinion, I have long entertained, that, in the civilization of savages, Military Discipline, or something nearly approaching it, may advantageously be employed.[13]

> In 1845 an enquiry was held in the Colony into the condition of the Aborigines. Giving evidence before the Committee, the Commissioner of Crown Lands for the Portland Bay District at Port Phillip claimed that a decrease in the Aboriginal population followed upon the arrival of the Protectors.

210   On my arrival here in 1837, I found scarcely an establishment in this neighbourhood without natives being employed thereon; many of them doing extremely well, and found useful; some acting as shepherds, and others in domestic uses; for these services they were well fed and clothed, and also well treated, and generally more kindly than the Europeans on the establishments. Immediately on the appearance of the Protectors, and missionary gentlemen, the natives left these employments; and I can have no hesitation in stating my opinion and firm conviction, that from the arrival of these parties, the aborigines in this district have declined any employment; lost sight of endeavouring to do any good for the community; wandering and pilfering through the country....[14]

> Another settler, answering the questions of Committee members, maintained that a belief in the harmfulness of the Protectorate was widespread.

211   *By Dr. Lang:* What is the general impression in the Port Phillip District as to the benefit derived by the public, from the establishment of the Protectorate? All that I have heard speak on the subject, say that the Protectorate has done more harm than good. *By the Chairman:* Is that impression universal in the district? I think so.
It is not confined to any particular party or parties in the District? No, I should say that is the universal impression.[15]

---

[13] Gipps to Stanley, 21 March 1844, *ibid.*, xxiii, pp. 497–8.
[14] Report from the Select Committee on the Condition of the Aborigines, *N.S.W.V.P.L.C.*, 1845, p. 44.
[15] Evidence of James Malcolm, Esq., *ibid.*, p. 15.

THE PROTECTORATE

In 1849 another Select Committee was appointed to look into the Protectorate itself. Written questions were forwarded to the Magistracy of the District, who tendered written evidence. The following letter, by a magistrate, has been chosen as typical of the prevailing opinions about the Protectorate, and illustrative of the settlers' hunger for land, which was always a barrier to those who tried to help the Aborigines. It was written by Edward Grimes, Commissioner of Crown Lands at Mount Macedon.

212 I have the honor to acknowledge the receipt of your communication of October 24, enclosing a Despatch from the Right Honorable the Secretary of State for the Colonies, respecting the future measures to be taken for the improvement of the condition of the Aboriginal Natives of the Colony.

As there are already two Reserves of the nature alluded to in this District, I conceive it to be unnecessary to point out any other localities for the above purposes, unless your Honor should consider that additional Reserves are called for.

I regret to observe that the suggestions of the Right Honorable the Secretary of State, appear to be based entirely upon the present Protectorate system, a system which I am firmly convinced, so far from attaining its desired end, has aggravated the very evils it was intended to remedy.

When the Protectorate Establishment was in full force, the distribution of rations to the Natives had the effect of increasing their naturally indolent habits, and the whole system encouraged a mutual jealousy between the Aborigines and the white settler, which was frequently attended with fatal results, while the attempts at education and moral improvement only resulted in a painful mockery of Religion.

There is no season of the year in this District, in which the Natives cannot procure abundant sustenance for themselves, and the facility is increased by the rapidly diminishing number of their tribes, while I am glad to state that a feeling of confidence and security has been established between the settlers and the Aborigines, which ensures the latter ready employment and ample recompense in rations and clothing, to all those who are willing to make themselves useful.

This improvement I attribute in a great measure to the cessation of any intercourse between the Natives and the Protectors, the Protectorate Station being notoriously the last place at which you are likely to meet any number of the Aborigines in this District.

From the wandering habits which are inherent in the Aborigines in this country, it is I think hopeless to expect to induce them to remain permanently in any one place, while I am certain that the cultivation of land, or the breeding of sheep by the Government for their benefit, would prove a most expensive means of attaining the desired end.

I should therefore suggest that the present Aboriginal Reserves, should be put up for public tender as sheep runs, and the funds derived from that source, together with the sum now uselessly expended on the Protectorate, should be devoted, under the direction of the Lord Bishop of Melbourne, to the formation of one or more schools for the younger population, who should be completely separated from their parents and their former habits, and these schools should be situated in the vicinity of Melbourne.

I am in hopes that from this system much good might eventually result, and the rising generation, so educated, might be induced at a later period to cultivate and reside upon the Reserves now made for their benefit.

I regret to state, that any attempt to reform or educate the Adult population, otherwise than is now being done by their gradual employment by the settlers, would in my opinion be utterly useless though it might be advisable, perhaps, to retain a small medical establishment on the site of the present Protectorate, to dispense medicines and provisions to the sick, the aged, and the infirm.[16]

> Commenting on the failure of the Protectorate system, C. J. La Trobe, Superintendent of Port Phillip, wrote to the New South Wales Colonial Secretary:

213 The cost of maintenance of the Protectorate, since its establishment, amounts to no less a sum than forty-two thousand two hundred pounds, and that of the Native Police to eleven thousand one hundred pounds—making a total expenditure of sixty-one thousand pounds in thirteen years.

The result of all this outlay may be stated in few words. Every one of these plans and arrangements made for the benefit of the Aboriginal Native, with exception of the last named, the Native Police, perhaps, has either completely failed, or shews at this date most undoubted signs of failure, in the attainment of the main objects aimed at.

The Protectorate, as I had occasion to state officially eighteen months ago, has totally failed to effect any of the higher and more important objects aimed at in its formation—and, I may again be allowed to repeat my opinion, that while it may not be justifiable to assert that it has been wholly inoperative, and has exercised no good influence upon the condition of the Aboriginal Native, still it may be believed, that if no such establishment had existed the state

---

[16] Appendix to the Report from the Select Committee on the Aborigines and Protectorate, *N.S.W.L.C.V.P.*, 1849, p. 12.

of the Aboriginal Native, within the District, would not have differed very greatly from what it now is—that the improved understanding to be remarked between the European settler and the Native is less the fruit of any influence which the Protectors have been in a position to exert, or have exerted, than of the altered position and circumstances of both parties, and the better appreciation that each possesses of the character and powers of the other.[17]

Later in his submission he attempted to explain this failure.

214   I have stated at the commencement of this communication, that the Protectorate had failed in the attainment of many of the principal objects aimed at by its establishment.

This failure must be mainly attributed to the impracticable nature of the scheme itself, and the inapplicability of the details, by which it was proposed to pursue it, to the real circumstances of the Aboriginal Natives of the Colony.

But I am necessitated to observe, that if no other cause were to be assigned for the failure of the Protectorate, to perform what was required, and what it promised, with respect to the Aborigines of this portion of the Australian Continent, the incongruous and ill-assorted character of the machinery employed, would furnish sufficient reason.

With regard to the office of Chief Protector, I must again repeat the conviction formerly expressed, that there was no occasion to employ an officer under such designation, and that there were no duties connected with the protection of the Natives in this District, nor any practicable arrangements for their improvement, which might not be carried out by a much less costly agency.

The further experience of the last year or eighteen months, has not only confirmed me in this opinion, but has further strengthened me in the conviction that the whole arrangement was a needlessly ponderous and expensive one; and that the sooner the scheme of the Protectorate, in its original or even present modified form, were abandoned, the better. I think it includes anomalies which will always prevent its satisfactory working.

The inquiry, in how far the individual character and conduct of Mr. Robinson may have influenced the result of the experiment mainly trusted to his supervision and management, is not easily answered. My own opinion is, that, if blame is to be attached, no much greater degree is to be ascribed to Mr. Robinson than to any of his assistants. They one and all have had their failings. They each, under one impulse or other, undertook, and had pretensions to a task beyond their powers. They never at any time drew together,

[17] 18 November 1848, *ibid.*, p. 4.

understood each other, or had mutual confidence, and there were many reasons to be given on all sides why it was hardly to be expected that any should exist.

Mr. Robinson was induced, and certainly under no ordinary circumstances of temptation, to undertake a duty for which he was totally unsuited. That he possessed some valuable natural or acquired qualifications for the work, will not be denied—but by withdrawing him from that position wherein under peculiar circumstances these had been developed, and by imposing upon him the task of bringing his past experience to bear upon a field of a different character after all, than that on which it had been gained,—through an agency, the management of which was quite beyond his powers,—his efficiency, such as it was, was destroyed. I must do him the justice to say, that if the work had been within his power, he would not have shrunk from its performance.[18]

> The Report of the 1849 Select Committee spelled the end of the Protectorate system.

215 Some of the evidence shews it to have been useless; while other witnesses state that its effect has been prejudicial to the objects of its care. One letter goes the length of asserting that the Protectors had thwarted the efforts of others to educate Aboriginal children. Your Committee are inclined to coincide in the two former opinions, but it must hesitate before they express their concurrence in the latter.

Your Committee regret that although they are compelled to advise the abolition of the present system, they are unable to recommend any other as a substitute. They cannot express any sanguine hopes as to the prospects of the adult population; and the education of the children, although proved to be practicable by success in isolated cases, is accompanied by difficulties, admitted by all acquainted with the subject, but which none have been able to surmount. The total separation of the parents from the children seems to be essential to the success of any plan, and your Committee believe that to effect this object compulsory measures would be required.

. . .

The total failure of all plans heretofore attempted, and the great expense already incurred, amounting, in thirteen years, to £61,000, induce your Committee to recommend that no hasty steps should be taken towards the introduction of a new system, until more mature consideration can be given to the subject. . . .[19]

---

[18] *Ibid.*, pp. 7-8.
[19] Report from the Select Committee on the Aborigines and Protectorate, *ibid.*, pp. 1, 2.

8
Aborigines and British Justice

The Aborigines' position as British subjects raised several complicated legal questions. These questions fell into three main areas.
1. Their inability to swear the accepted Christian oath made it impossible for them to give testimony in the courts of law.
2. They were acknowledged as British subjects answerable to British law; but did this give the white men the right to interfere when Aborigines committed crimes against other Aborigines? Or should the law accept a parallel existence of tribal law under which these actions were not 'crimes'?
3. Aborigines' ignorance of the workings of the law, coupled with language barriers and their illiteracy, militated against their using the law for their own defence.

This chapter examines some of the episodes where the problems of the Aborigines and British justice were raised. At least one of the three main problems outlined above was involved in each episode, but more often the other two issues were also present.

One of the earliest cases occurred in 1799, and revealed not only the difficulty of gaining evidence of white atrocities against natives, but also the problem the Governor faced when the judiciary were, in his opinion, too lenient on the whites. Governor Hunter wrote of the case to England.

216 Two native boys have lately been most barbarously murder'd by several of the settlers at the Hawkesbury River, notwithstanding Orders have upon this subject been repeatedly given pointing out in what instances only they were warranted in punishing with such severity. The above two youths had been in the habit of being much with the settlers, but from the manner in which this shocking murder was perpetrated I judg'd it highly necessary to have the murderers taken immediately into custody, and a court was instantly ordered for their trial. The court having unanimously found the prisoners guilty of killing two natives, were divided with respect to the nature of the sentence, as your Grace will discover by the trial, which is herewith, sent at the instance of the majority of the court. The manner in which this decision appears to have been come to, I conceive, my Lord, not to have been correct. I am of opinion that a reference to His Majesty's Minister shou'd have been recommended by the court to the Governor, and not from the court directly and independantly of the Commander-in-Chief, because the power either to approve and confirm or to moderate the severity of any criminal sentence is delegated by His Majesty to him.

Those men found guilty of murder are now at large and living upon their farms, as much at their ease as ever. I conceive, from the nature of the Governor's authority, I might have rejected the bail and kept the prisoners under confinement until the effect of the special reference was known; but I have been unwilling to shew to the colony that any difference is likely to take place between the judicial and executive authoritys, particularly when in the smallest degree inconsistent with lenity. If I am mistaken in my ideas upon the above trial, I hope and request to be instructed.

You will discover, my Lord, what a host of evidence is brought forward from that quarter to prove what numbers of white people have been kill'd by the natives; but cou'd we have brought with equal ease such proofs from the natives as they are capable of affording of the wanton and barbarous manner in which many of them have been destroy'd, and to have confronted them with those of the white inhabitants, we shou'd have found an astonishing difference in the numbers. Every information within my power respecting the light in which the natives of this country were to be held as a people now under the protection of His Majesty's Government was laid before the court. The Order given upon that subject, both before my time and since, was made known to it. I also laid before its members an article in His Majesty's instructions to the Governor, which is strong and expressive, and is as follows ... [Here follows an extract from the Instructions to Governors; see Document 3, above.]

The intentions of His Majesty from this part of the Governor's Instructions are clear and evident. The above cruel act is the second which I have brought before a Court of Criminal Judicature in order to prevent, as far as in my power, this horrid practice of wantonly destroying the natives. Much of that hostile disposition which has occasionally appear'd in those people has been but too often provoked by the treatment which many of them have received from the white inhabitants, and which have scarsely been heard of by those who have the power of bestowing punishment.[1]

Governor King, vexed by the continued hostilities between the settlers and the Aborigines, in 1805 asked Judge-Advocate Atkins for his opinions

[1] Hunter to Portland, 2 January 1800, *H.R.A.*, I, ii, pp. 401–2.

on the matter. Atkins, in his reply, was largely concerned with the question of whether the evidence of persons unable to swear on oath could be accepted as legal. However, it is interesting to note that he did not feel that a lack of legal evidence should prevent white men from inflicting punishment on the Aborigines.

217   In obedience to your Excellency's injunctions to me, I have given the two paragraphs in the letter of His Majesty's Secretary of State to the Executive Government of this colony, respecting the treatment of the natives, all the consideration in my power. I have further read the whole of the correspondence of Mr. Arndell and others with your Excellency, stating the outrages committed by the natives of the Hawkesbury, and I am now to give my opinion thereon, which I do with the greatest deference.

It is in vain to make it a question from whence those excesses originated—from the inherent brutality of the natives, or from real or supposed injuries they may have sustained from the settlers. It becomes more the object to consider of the best method to prevent it in future. And here two paths naturally present themselves—that of rigor or lenity. If the first is purposed, can it be done legally? I mean, can it be done conformable to the existing law? I think it cannot, for the evidence of persons not bound by any moral or religious tie, can never be considered or construed as legal evidence. Your Excellency well knows that the members of the Court of Criminal Judicature are sworn to "give a true verdict according to the *evidence*"; and however strong the necessity of making public examples of the offending natives may appear, can it supersede that obligation on their (the members') consciences? And should the members of the Court apply to me for my opinion as Judge-Advocate, can I say it is legal and according to law? The natives are within the pale of His Majesty's protection; but how can a native, when brought to trial, plead guilty or not guilty to an indictment, the meaning and tendency of which they must be totally ignorant of? Plead they must, before evidence can be adduced against them, and penal laws cannot be stretched to answer a particular exigency.

. . .

The object of this letter is to impress the idea that the natives of this country (generally speaking) are at present incapable of being brought before a Criminal Court, either as criminals or as evidences; that it would be a mockery of judicial proceedings, and a solecism in law; and that the only mode at present, when they deserve it, is to pursue and inflict such punishment as they may merit.[2]

---

[2] Atkins to King, 8 July 1805, *H.R.N.S.W.*, pp. 653, 654.

The difficulty of accepting unsworn testimony was not solved in New South Wales until over seventy years after Judge-Advocate Atkins raised the objection.

In the meantime the various governors did what they could to prevent hostilities between black and white, and in particular to lessen white outrages committed against Aborigines. Earl Bathurst questioned one aspect of Governor Darling's efforts in this direction, for he saw Darling's recommendations as leading to even greater difficulties, and to an increase in hostilities. In 1826 he wrote to Darling:

218   I have had the honour to receive your dispatch, No. 28 of the 6th of May last, transmitting the Copy of a Government notice, which you had felt it necessary to issue on the occasion of an outrage committed by the Natives of two Stock keepers in the County of Argyle.

I have much pleasure in conveying to you His Majesty's Approbation of the course, which you have adopted to prevent a recurrence of similar proceedings, as much to be deplored on account of the Individual cases of violence, which have unfortunately resulted, as from the general alarm, which the assemblage of so large a body of people must create throughout the Colony.

There is, however, one part of the Regulations, the policy of which I am much disposed to question. I allude to the encouragement directed to be held out to the Natives by the promise of Rewards "to seize and deliver up any Men, who shall ill-treat them, in order that they may be punished for such offence." As it is not to the principle of Rewards, but to the seizure of the person of the Offenders, to which I am adverse, I have no wish to alter that part of the Regulation, further than as respects the particular point, to which I have adverted; my objection, therefore, will be removed, if, for the words "to secure and deliver up any Men, who shall ill-treat them," you were to substitute the following, vizt. "to furnish such information as may lead to their detection."

Unless this alteration be made, I am apprehensive that the permission to the Natives to secure any person, by whom they may consider themselves aggrieved, may of itself lead to that very evil, which it is the object of the Regulation to remedy, or for the sake of the reward induce them to lay hold of innocent persons, or others whose offences may not be of that character, as to require the infliction of any severe punishment.[3]

Commenting on the report of an attack made on Aborigines by an exploring party under Major Mitchell on 27 May 1836, Lord Glenelg

[3] Bathurst to Darling, 3 October 1826, *H.R.A.*, I, xii, pp. 600–601

reiterated in a letter to Bourke that Australian Aborigines were subjects of the Crown, with all the rights that this involved.

219   It is happily superfluous for me to impress upon you the general principles to be observed in your conduct towards the Aborigines. I shall soon be enabled to transmit to you the Report of the Committee of the House of Commons on this subject made before the close of the present Session, and I have reason to suppose that you will there find the result of much diligent enquiry and reflection. For the present, therefore, I confine myself to remarks, which may perhaps appear to proceed on a less comprehensive view of the subject than under the circumstances I should have thought it right at least to attempt.

Your Commission as Governor of N. S. Wales asserts H. M.'s Sovereignty over every part of the Continent of New Holland which is not embraced in the Colonies of Western or Southern Australia. Hence I conceive it follows that all the natives inhabiting those Territories must be considered as Subjects of the Queen, and as within H. M.'s Allegiance. To regard them as Aliens with whom a War can exist, and against whom H. M.'s Troops may exercise belligerent right, is to deny that protection to which they derive the highest possible claim from the Sovereignty which has been assumed over the whole of their Ancient Possessions. I am well aware that legal maxims of this kind will not serve for the solution of practical difficulties such as those in which Major Mitchell was involved, and that, in extreme Exigencies of that nature, Public Officers are not to be governed altogether by Ordinary rules. At the same time it appears to me necessary that those rules should be steadily borne in mind in estimating the apology made for an occasional departure from them. If the rights of the Aborigines as British Subjects be fully acknowledged, it will follow that, when any of them comes to his death by the hands of the Queen's Officers, or of persons acting under their Command, an Inquest should be held to ascertain the cause which lead to the Death of the deceased. Such a proceeding is important not only as a direct protection to Society at large against lawless Outrage, but as it impresses on the Public a just estimate of the value of Human Life. I am of course aware that in such a case as the present it would have been impossible to hold an inquisition before the Coroner. But I am not satisfied that a proceeding identical in principle, and corresponding to a certain extent even in form, might not have been advantageously taken. For example, Such of the Justices of the Peace as hold Commissions extending over the whole Colony might, I apprehend, have been required to hold a public enquiry into the circumstances which occasioned the Deaths of the Aborigines, and to report the result to you. An impressive lesson might, it should seem, have thus been given of the importance attached by the Government to the Life of a Native, and the exculpation of Major Mitchell would have been more satisfactory both to the Public at large and to himself. If it should be objected that such a proceeding would have been in any sense of the term an indignity, I would reply that to be furnished with an opportunity of removing a reproach incurred in the discharge of a public duty is not usually regarded as injurious by any man, either in Civil or Military Life, and that the respect for public opinion by which Our Countrymen are distinguished reconciles them to such investigations, while the prevailing sense of justice affords an ample security on such occasions even against the Current of popular prejudice.[4]

> The Report of the House of Commons Select Committee referred to in the above Despatch from Lord Glenelg made several comments on the rights of native peoples under British jurisdiction. The rights of the Aborigines under British law were made clear:

220 ... and by the commissions under which the Australian Colonies are governed Her Majesty's sovereignty over the whole of New Holland is asserted without reserve. It follows, therefore, that the Aborigines of the whole territory must be considered as within the allegiance of the Queen, and as entitled to her protection. Whatever may have been the injustice of this encroachment, there is no reason to suppose that either justice or humanity would now be consulted by receding from it. On the contrary, it would appear eminently desirable to impress upon the Australian Government, and upon the inhabitants of those Colonies, the consequences of the principles upon which they have been thus founded. If the whole of New Holland be part of the British Empire, then every inhabitant of that vast island is under the defence of British law as often as his life or property may be attacked; and the appeal to arms for adjusting controversies with any part of the primitive race, exposes those by whom blood may be shed to the same responsibility, and to the same penalities, as if the sufferers were white persons.[5]

> Recognizing the complications involved, the Committee recommended that the Protectors and other officials on the spot, who were familiar with the situation, should try to work out some solution.

221 To require from the ignorant hordes of savages living in Eastern or Western Australia the observance of our laws would be

---

[4] Glenelg to Bourke, 26 July 1837, *ibid.*, xix, pp. 48-9.
[5] Report from the Select Committee on Aborigines (British Settlements), *loc. cit.*, p. 83.

absurd, and to punish their non-observance of them by severe penalties would be palpably unjust. On the other hand, if they are placed beyond the pale of the law as a rule of their conduct to others, they will infallibly lose the advantage of it, considered as a rule of conduct of others towards them. To determine under what special regulations they should be placed, is a task to be performed only by those who can study the question with the aid of the most minute and close local observation. It should therefore be one branch of the duty of the Protectors to suggest to the local Government, and through it to the local Legislature, such short and simple rules as may form a temporary and provisional code for the regulation of the Aborigines, until advancing knowledge and civilization shall have superseded the necessity for any such special laws.[6]

> Others were deeply concerned at the obvious disparity between the Aborigines' rights as British subjects, and their lack of protection under the law. Benjamin Hurst, a missionary in the Port Phillip District, wrote to La Trobe, the Superintendent of the District:

222 The Aborigines are declared to be British subjects, and it therefore appears to me are entitled to the protection of British law. But there is in my apprehension something peculiar in the case of the Tautgort Tribe. Two years ago, this Tribe was a numerous one, but nearly the whole of the fighting men have been butchered in cold blood by Europeans, so that they are so far reduced as to be unable to defend themselves against the inroads of the neighbouring Tribes. In both the murders committed here a Tautgort has been the victim, and I believe from no other cause than that their number is now so small that they dare not seek to be revenged. I feel persuaded Your Honor will agree with me in thinking this is a case which demands the serious attention of the Government, especially as in the present state of the law the guilty parties cannot be brought to punishment.[7]

> The lack of understanding of the Aborigines' rights as British subjects was demonstrated by the story of the Myall Creek Massacre (see Chapter 3). The white defendants' claim that they thought it hard that white men should be executed for killing blacks, and Gipps' belief that the man never thought their lives were in jeopardy, clearly illustrate how white men believed the law to stand fifty years after the beginning of settlement.
>   Another pronouncement made in the Report handed down in 1837 by the Select Committee on Aborigines concerned those instances where native custom and usage involved actions against other natives which were criminal in the eyes of the British:

[6] *Ibid.*, p. 84.
[7] Hurst to La Trobe, 22 July 1841, Bonwick Transcripts, Box 54, M.L.

223 ... when the British law is violated by the Aborigines within the British dominions, it seems right that the utmost indulgence compatible with a due regard for the lives and properties of others, should be shown for their ignorance and prejudices. Actions which they have been taught to regard as praiseworthy we consider as meriting the punishment of death. It is of course impossible to adopt or sanction the barbarous notions which have urged the criminal to the commission of the offence, but neither is it just to exclude them from our view in awarding the punishment of his crime.[8]

> This was another aspect touched on by the missionary Hurst. In his letter to La Trobe, he told of a raid made on the Mission by some 200 natives in order to avenge the death from disease of an elderly man some months previously. It had been the second such act of revenge that year.

224 I am not aware that in the present state of the law any thing can be done in this particular instance to punish the murderers, especially as the evidence of Aborigines cannot be received in Court; but I would beg respectfully to suggest whether it is not advisable both for the Home and Colonial Government to adopt such measures as would in the mildest but most effectual manner prevent the different Tribes from making aggressions upon each other. I am aware that some philanthropists think we ought not to interfere with the political arrangements of the Natives, and were I less intimately connected with them than I am, I too should probably think the same. But living among them as we do, and being acquainted with their manners and customs (at least to some considerable extent) it is the opinion both of my Colleague and myself, that unless the Government interferes in order to protect those who may be disposed to remain at any establishment formed for their benefit, their civilization will be very considerably retarded.[9]

> Hurst advocated more lenient punishment for crimes by Aborigines against Aborigines.

225 With regard to the degree of punishment to be inflicted upon a Native who injures or kills another, it should, particularly in the first instance, be much less than would be inflicted upon an European for the like offence. If the punishment were made certain, and without reference to the period that might elapse between the commission of the crime and the apprehension of the guilty indi-

---

[8] Report of the Select Committee on Aborigines (British Settlements), *loc. cit.*, p. 80.
[9] Hurst to La Trobe, 22 July 1841, Bonwick Transcripts, Box 54, M.L.

vidual, a mild measure would operate much more beneficially than a severe one and less certain punishment.[10]

> The question of whether Aborigines could be tried in British courts for crimes against other Aborigines was reopened in September 1841 at a hearing of the Supreme Court of the Port Phillip District.

226   In the month of Septt. last, an Aboriginal Native was brought to trial before the Supreme Court of the Port Phillip District for the murder of another Aboriginal in the immediate vicinity of Melbourne.

The Counsel employed for the accused raised a question as to the jurisdiction of the Court; and Mr. Justice Willis, though he decided that the trial should go on, expressed very strongly his doubts of the competency of the Court to try the Aborigines for offences committed *inter se*, and stated that, in the event of the accused being found guilty, he would reserve the point.

Had the trial proceeded and the man been found guilty, the point would have been brought solemnly for discussion before a full Court in Sydney; but, as the Crown Prosecutor on the failure of some expected evidence entered a *nolle prosequi*, the trial did not go on; consequently there has been no case for argument before the full Court; and the opinions expressed by Mr. Justice Willis have produced a very general impression in the Colony, and especially at Port Phillip, that the Aborigines are not amenable to our Courts of Justice for offences committed *inter se*, though they may be, as Mr. Willis (I believe) admits, for offences committed on the persons of white men, or of any others not being Aboriginal Natives.

Considering any such uncertainty as to the state of the Law to be very inconvenient, it occurred to me that it would be proper to remove all doubt by passing an Act of Council, declaring the Aborigines to be amenable to our Laws in all cases wherein those Laws could be applied; but, before I adopted such a measure, I thought it right to consult the Judges as to the necessity and propriety of it. I accordingly caused the letter, of which a Copy is enclosed, to be written to the Chief Justice; and, in reply, I received one from His Honor, of which I also enclose a copy, conveying to me the opinion of the Judges that the Aborigines are amenable to our Laws; and, pointing out the occasion on which, after a solemn argument, it was decided that they were so amenable in the year 1836; further

[10] *Ibid.*

also stating that, in the opinion of their Honors, no declaratory Law upon the subject is necessary.[11]

> In order to make the position quite clear, Gipps decided to put a Bill before the Legislative Council, but before doing so he sought the advice of the judges on the matter of crimes committed by Aborigines against their own people. Colonial Secretary Thomson wrote on Gipps' behalf, in the following terms:

227 Sir George Gipps desires me to add that He thinks it right (although not with any view of biassing the opinion of the Judges) to state briefly the grounds, on which He considers the Aborigines to be in all respects amenable to our Laws.

1. The Sovereigns of Great Britain have for more than half a Century assumed unqualified dominion over the parts of New Holland forming the Territory of New South Wales, and have exercised unqualified dominion wherever their authority has been established.

2. It has been ordained by an Act of Parliament, 9 Geo. IV. C. 83. that, within the Colony of New South Wales, British Law shall be established without reference to any other Law or Laws, save such as may be made by the Local Legislature.

3. That, in numerous official documents issued under the immediate sanction of Her Majesty, the Aborigines of this Country are called Her Majesty's subjects, and declared to be entitled to the same protection as any other Class of Her Majesty's subjects.

4. That, upon British Territory, no Law save British Law can prevail, except by virtue of some Treaty or Enactment; and no such Treaty or Enactment has ever been made, either with or in respect to the Aborigines of New South Wales.

5. That, even if the Aborigines be looked upon as a conquered people, and it be even further admitted that a conquered People are entitled to preserve their own Laws until a different Law be proclaimed by the Conqueror, still no argument in favor of a separate Code of Laws for the Aborigines of New South Wales can be drawn therefrom, first, because the Aborigines never have been in possession of any Code of Laws intelligible to a Civilized People, and secondly, because their Conquerors (if the Sovereigns of Great Britain are so to be considered) have declared that British Law shall prevail throughout the whole Territory of New South Wales.

In conclusion, His Excellency directs me to state to your Honor that, although He thus contends that British Law alone exists in the Colony, He entirely admits that, in putting the Law in force

---

[11] Gipps to Stanley, 24 January 1842, *H.R.A.*, I, xxi, pp. 653-4.

against the Aborigines, the utmost degree of Mercy and forbearance should be exercised.[12]

> Judge Dowling's reply was based on precedents in the Colony which he and other members of the Bench considered before reaching the conclusion that Aborigines were amenable to English law.

228 Having had a conference with my Brother Judges on this subject, I have the honor to inform your Excellency that the question submitted for our consideration has already been judicially determined by the Supreme Court, after solemn argument on a Plea to the Jurisdiction, the Judges holding that the Aborigines of New South Wales are amenable to British Law in the Courts of this Colony for offences against the Public peace committed on each other.

It is true that, soon after my arrival in the Colony in 1828, I found an opinion prevailing that the Supreme Court could not take cognizance of offences committed amongst the Aborigines, and, in one or two instances, the Court, from the difficulty of administering Justice between them according to the Rules of English Law, forbore trying those individual cases. The question of Jurisdiction was not however argued at the Bar, and from the great infrequency of such cases, the course taken was silently adopted from conformity, rather with the impression prevailing, than as the result of deliberate Judgment.[13]

> In reply to Gipps' queries on the matter, Lord Stanley stated that it was superfluous for him to submit the question to the Attorney-General and the Solicitor General:

229 ... the question has been already solemnly decided on argument in the year 1836 by the Supreme Court, in opposition to the views entertained by Mr. Willis; and, until that decision is over-ruled, I conclude it must be held to be the Law of the Colony. I understand also that the Judges of the Supreme Court, with the exception of Mr. Willis, are individually of opinion that the decision in 1836 was correct; that they have no doubt of the Law; that a similar Case argued before them on Appeal would in all probability be similarly ruled; and that they see no occasion for the declaratory Law.

Under these circumstances, I must hold them to be the best and most competent Judges, and must decline to refer the Case for the opinion of the Attorney and Solicitor General.[14]

---

[12] Thomson to Dowling, 4 January 1842, *ibid.*, pp. 655–6.
[13] Dowling to Gipps, 8 January 1842, *ibid.*, p. 656.
[14] Stanley to Gipps, 2 July 1842, *ibid.*, xxii, p. 133.

We return now to the question of Aboriginal evidence being inadmissable because it had to be unsworn. Benjamin Hurst was among those who saw that a solution must be reached.

230   They may be destroyed by their fellows, and what is worse, may be shot by wholesale by Europeans, and yet the arm of the law has no power to punish unless the evidence of a white person can be procured. To meet their case I would respectfully suggest the propriety of allowing the Aborigines to give evidence in Court whether a Native or an European be the offending party. I readily admit that their testimony should be received with caution from the circumstances of their not being fully acquainted with the solemn obligations of an oath, but at the same time I am of opinion that when it is corroborated by circumstantial evidence it should be received. Nor do I see how they can be protected, or how justice can be done to them, unless some provision be made to meet their case in this respect.[15]

In July 1839, the Aborigines' Protection Society (an offshoot of the humanitarian movement) presented a statement to the Marquis of Normanby concerning the admission of the evidence of Aborigines in the courts of law.

231   Amongst various points which have engaged the attention of the Aborigines Protection Society as necessary to ensure the safety and elevation of the uncivilized Natives of those parts of the Globe, on which British Colonies or Settlements are formed, the subject of their admission to give Evidence in Our Courts of Law has repeatedly excited particular interest.

It is evident that the rejection of the Evidence of these Natives renders them virtually outlaws in their Native Land which they have never alienated or forfeited. It seems to be a moral impossibility that their existence can be maintained when in the state of weakness and degradation, which their want of civilization necessarily implies: they have to cope with some of the most cruel and atrocious of our species, who carry on their system of oppression with almost perfect impunity so long as the Evidence of Native Witnesses is excluded from Our Courts.

The attention of the Committee of the Aborigines' Protection Society has been again called to this subject by a Letter from Barton Hack, Esquire, one of their corresponding Members at Adelaide, a Settlement which stands preeminent amongst Our Colonies for the better feeling which it has fostered towards the Native population. That letter contains the particulars of a case in which the practical difficulty has been exhibited, accompanied

[15] Hurst to La Trobe, 22 July 1841, Bonwick Transcripts, Box 54, M.L.

with the expression of urgent desire that the remedy might be applied by the admission of Native Evidence.

For the purpose of obtaining the removal of this very serious inability from the Native population of Our Australian Colonies and of thereby securing at least one step towards their elevation, the Aborigines' Protection Society have had a Bill prepared which they hoped would be passed with the concurrence and support of Her Majesty's Government.

Intimation however having reached the Committee of the Society that the course which it was prepared to take did not meet the approbation of the Colonial office, it has determined to suspend the further prosecution of the Bill and again address the Colonial Office in the hope that the appeal, which they now offer, limited as it is to the subject of Evidence and confined to the Aborigines of Australia or to the Australians and the Islands of the Pacific, will not be made in vain. The Committee cannot but anticipate that the effectual carrying out of measures, calculated to secure the object which the Bill in question was destined to obtain, will prove so real a boon to the Native population and so important to the respectable Class of British Emigrants, so decided a check to evil doers, and so satisfactory to the friends of humanity in this Country, that it may be speedily followed up by similar measures applicable to all the Courts in Our Colonies and Dependencies.[16]

> This statement was forwarded to Mr Justice Burton (one of the Judges of the Supreme Court of New South Wales), who was asked to say whether, in fact, any objection had ever been made to the admission of the evidence of Aborigines in the Courts of New South Wales. Burton told the Under Secretary of State of two factors making Aboriginal evidence inadmissible.

232 In answer to your letter of this date [17 August 1839], requesting me to state for the information of the Marquess of Normanby whether any objection has ever been made to admit the evidence of the Aborigines in the Court of New South Wales, and if so in what manner I conceive that defect in the administration of Justice could be most properly remedied. I have the honor to state that objections have certainly been made and sustained by the Supreme Courts of New South Wales to the admission of such evidence, but only on the two following grounds. First, where it has been impossible to communicate with a proposed witness on account of his ignorance of the English Language, and where no Interpreter could be procured to interpret between him and the

---

[16] *H.R.A.*, xx, pp. 303–4.

Court; Secondly, where a proposed witness has been found to be ignorant of a Supreme Being and a future State.

The defect arising from these causes, it is obvious can only be remedied by religious instruction.

Whether it is expedient to introduce into the Australian Colonies any modification of the English Law of Evidence now existing there is however involved in His Lordship's Enquiry, and I conceive that, in certain cases where the matter at issue is of minor consideration, the statements of the Aborigines might be received as evidence; and I had the honor of preparing a Bill for their Protection in New South Wales, in which that principle is recognized and acted upon; it was transmitted by me to His Excellency the Governor, Sir Geo. Gipps, together with a letter explanatory of its intention in the Month of June, 1838, but was not laid as I hoped it would be by His Excellency before the Legislative Council in consequence, as I presumed, of a recommendation of the Committee of the House of Commons, that no measure of that kind should be of Colonial Origin.

My rough Draft of the Bill referred to and a copy of my Letter to Sir Geo. Gipps have been already transmitted by me to you. I conceive that it is a measure, which would give satisfaction to the Friends of the Aborigines both in England and in the Colony, if it were adopted.

Respecting cases which are of a degree of importance higher than those contemplated in that Bill, I am of opinion that no alteration in the Law should be made.[17]

As a result of this letter, Normanby instructed Gipps to overcome the difficulties outlined by Mr Justice Burton, by submitting legislation to the Council.

233 It appears that Mr. Burton has already brought this subject under your consideration, and it seems to me desirable that you should submit to the Legislative Council some well digested plan for obviating such impediments as prevent the admission of the testimony of the Aborigines in Judicial proceedings.

So far as that obstacle arises from the inability of the Court to understand their language or ascertain their meaning through an Interpreter, it is of course irremediable by Legislation, and can be overcome only by instructing them in the English Language, or by engaging some competent person to study theirs. But so far as the rejection of their testimony is founded on their want of religious knowledge, and of the sanctions by which Religion forbids the violation of truth in Judicial testimony, as this is at present the

---

[17] Burton to Labouchere, 17 August 1839, *ibid.*, pp. 304–5.

inevitable result of that barbarous ignorance in which they have lived from their birth, the absolute rejection of the testimony on such grounds would appear to be injurious to the interests of Justice. But the ultimate remedy must at the same time be unceasingly sought in an improved system of moral and religious instruction.[18]

> However, the Act passed by the Legislative Council proved unacceptable, as may be seen from the following statement made by the Attorney-General and the Solicitor General to the Secretary of State, Lord John Russell:

234 Having duly considered the Act passed by the Legislative Council of New South Wales "to allow the Aboriginal Natives of New South Wales to be received as competent witnesses in Criminal Cases," transmitted to us by your Lordship's directions, we have to report to your Lordship that in our opinion it cannot properly be submitted to The Queen for confirmation.

To admit in a Criminal case the evidence of a witness acknowledged to be ignorant of the existence of a God or a future state ould be contrary to the principles of British jurisprudence: and the Act is loosely worded with respect to the admission of such evidence and the weight to be given to it that we do not think it could be attended with any advantage.

We should have supposed that the Aboriginal Natives might have been sufficiently instructed before being produced as witnesses to render their evidence admissable according to the established rules of Law, which do not define the distinctness of Religious ideas or to what degree the belief in a future state is to be fixed to qualify a witness to take an Oath.[19]

> Gipps thought that the disallowance of the New South Wales Act had mixed results, so far as the Aborigines were concerned.

235 It is true that in administering the Law, and especially in enforcing the penalties of it, a difference is frequently made between Savages (who understand it not) and persons of European origin; but this difference is invariably in favor of the Savage; and, if it were not so, the Law would become the instrument of the most grievous injustice.

It is only the more obvious offences against Society than can with any degree of justice be visited against the Savage with extreme severity, such as Murder, rape, violence against the person, and other offences, which there can be no doubt should be regarded

---
[18] Normanby to Gipps, 31 August 1839, *ibid.*, pp. 302–3.
[19] Campbell and Wilde to Russell, 27 July 1840, *ibid.*, p. 756.

alike by the Savage and the civilized man, as deserving of punishment.

It seems to me however right to point out to Your Lordship that the inadmissibility of their evidence acts perhaps quite as often in favor of the Aborigines as against them. The hardship of the exclusion of evidence, that might be favorable to them, is always urged on the Jury both by their Counsel and by the Judge; and is again taken into consideration by the Executive in carrying into effect the judgment of the Court. The admission indeed of their evidence was, in 1839, as much called for in New South Wales by parties who had suffered from the aggressions of the Blacks, as by those who advocate their civilization; and complaints have long been loud amongst our Settlers that, whilst the penalties of the Law are rigorously enforced against persons who commit violence on the Aborigines, the Aborigines themselves are, when brought into our Courts, almost invariably acquitted.

This has operated, there is some reason to believe, very unfavorably for the Aborigines, as, from the difficulty and uncertainty of bringing them to justice, there is a disposition, engendered in the minds of the less principled portion of the White population, to take the law into their own hands, as was the case when nearly three years ago not less than 28 aboriginal natives were barbarously murdered in the Liverpool Plains District; an act of atrocity for which however seven White Men paid the forfeit of their lives on the Scaffold.

I have further to observe that Counsel is usually assigned by the Supreme Court to any Natives brought for trial before it; and that the Government always provides the attendance of Interpreters, when they can possibly be found. Mr. Threlkeld, a Missionary of the London Society, has usually acted on such occasions; and he must, I doubt not, consider it his business to protect the Natives as well as to interpret for them.

I have moreover very recently, on the application of the Chief Justice, appointed a standing Counsel for the Aborigines, who will receive a fixed payment from the Government for every case in which he is engaged. The fee is to be three Guineas for every case in Sydney, and five Guineas in the Country.[20]

> Mr Threlkeld, mentioned in the above document, had been for some years acting as interpreter for Aborigines brought to Court. So frequently did this duty need to be performed, that the Registrar of the Supreme Court was given permission to employ the Missionary in this capacity whenever necessary, without gaining special permission each time.

[20] Gipps to Russell, 7 April 1841, *ibid.*, xxi, pp. 313-14.

236   To obviate the necessity of obtaining a special authority every time that the Reverend Mr. Threlkeld attends the Supreme Court as Interpreter to the Aborigines, I do myself the honor to convey to you the Sanction of His Excellency the Governor to your including that Gentleman's name in Your Contingent Abstract for the Sum of Five Pounds, for every case in which he may produce the Crown Solicitor's Certificate of his having been subpone'd and duly attended in the above capacity.[21]

> The main point of Gipps' Despatch of April 1841—the inadmissibility of Aboriginal evidence—was given consideration by the British Government in 1843. An Act was passed by Parliament, and sent to Gipps to be placed before the Legislative Council.

237   I transmit to you, herewith, a copy of an Act of Parliament, which has recently been passed to authorize the Legislatures of Certain of Her Majesty's Colonies to pass Laws for the admission, in certain Cases, of unsworn testimony in Civil and Criminal proceedings, the object being to provide for the admission of the Evidence of Aboriginal Natives. The circumstances, which have given rise to the passing of this Act, have been so fully entered into in previous correspondence that it is only necessary for me now to instruct you to propose to the Legislative Council of New South Wales a Law for giving effect to the provisions of the Act of Parliament.[22]

> On Gipps' instructions, a Bill was framed to give effect to the provisions of the British Act. However, under the colony's new constitution, proclaimed in 1842, the Bill was required to come before a legislative council which comprised an elected majority. This Council, dominated by wealthy landowners generally hostile to the British government and the colonial executive, threw out the Bill. One member of the Council, Sir Thomas Mitchell, himself a government officer, reflected the view of a majority of members.

238   The framers of the Act of Parliament under the sanction of which the present Bill was brought in, were unacquainted with the nature of the people about whom they were legislating; but he, who was better versed in their habits, would venture to affirm that it would be impossible to depend upon arriving at the truth through the medium of their evidence. The whole study of their lives was how they should best conceal the workings of their minds from the eye of the observer; and to receive the evidence of such witnesses would

---

[21] Assistant Colonial Secretary Harington to Registrar of the Supreme Court, 10 June 1838, W. W. Burton, Papers Relating to Aborigines 1796–1891, MS. no. A1161, M.L.
[22] Stanley to Gipps, 6 July 1843, *H.R.A.*, I, xxiii, p. 9.

be to affect most vitally the security of the whole country. Another fact with which the framers of the Act could not have been aware was that the members of every tribe stood in the same degree of relationship towards each other as brothers and sisters among a Christian community, and therefore were not in a position likely to induce them to give fair and impartial testimony.[23]

> Five years later another attempt was made to introduce a Bill 'almost in the very words' of the 1844 Bill. Again it was defeated. The two following extracts from the *Sydney Morning Herald*'s report of the debate illustrate the strong anti-native sentiments that were expressed by members of the Council.

239 Mr. FOSTER rose to object to the Bill and he did so because he thought it would be impossible to place any safeguard on the evidence of the blacks. They were so utterly debased a race, that they had no knowledge of truth or falsehood. The vices of our race were with them virtues, and our virtues vices. If a black took the life of one of a hostile tribe, he considered it a virtuous action, and they looked on the whites as a hostile tribe. But if even the whites took the lives of blacks of one tribe, those of another hostile to the slain applauded the whites for it. . . . It was admitted by all that the minds of this race were incapable of entertaining one scintilla of anything like religion, and how was it possible they should be restrained from giving false testimony.[24]

Mr Nichols saw no point in impeding the 'march of civilization'.

240 There was no doubt that the blacks had been very much neglected and ill-treated by the Government of this country: but they were a most debased and degraded race, and their desires extended only for trifling matters. He found in one report from the Government that the utmost ambition of the king of a tribe was "to have a long-tailed coat, a cocked hat, and to be a swell." (Laughter.) There was no doubt that such a race as this must give way before the march of civilization; they could not be instructed, and must eventually perish from the earth, as white men approached to occupy it.[25]

> The last word must be accorded to William Charles Wentworth, who expressed so clearly the colonial resentment of British interference in matters which could not possibly concern them. The people of Exeter Hall (a London meeting place for several missionary groups) were accused of undue influence. Wentworth believed that the measure:

---

[23] Report of Legislative Council proceedings, 20 June 1844, in *Sydney Morning Herald*, 21 June 1844.
[24] *Ibid.*, 29 June 1849.
[25] *Ibid.*

241   ... was not in its ultimate source to be regarded either as the act of the Minister, of the vote of Parliament, but the pervading influence of that clique who had for years past wrought the destinies of the colony for evil—the influence of Exeter Hall. (Cheers.) ... There it was that this measure had its root; from thence it sprung and passed through Parliament aided in its gestative growth only by the recipients of the salaries and the conductors of the powers of that institution. (Here here.) The Act on which this Bill was founded, was introduced into the House in silence; it had been passed in silence, under the influence, the dominant influence, to which he had before alluded, and which for twenty years past had been the bane of the colonies.

... he denied the policy of Government interference in this matter altogether. He could not see if the whites in this colony were to go out into the land and possess it, that the Government had much to do with them. No doubt there would be battles between the settlers and the border tribes; but they might be settled without the aid of the Government. The civilized people had come in and the savage must go back. (Cheers.) They must go on progressing until their dominancy was established, and therefore he could think that no measure was wise or merciful to the blacks which clothed them with a degree of seeming protection, which their position would not allow them to maintain. ... It was not the policy of a wise Government to attempt the perpetuation of the aboriginal race of New South Wales by any protective means. They must give way before the arms, aye! even the diseases of civilized nations— they must give way before they attain the power of those nations.[26]

> Thus, in 1850, Aborigines were regarded as British subjects without the full rights that this entailed; amenable to British laws, but unable to give evidence in British courts.[27]

---

[26] *Ibid.*
[27] It was not, in fact, until 1876 that the Aborigines of New South Wales attained the right to give unsworn evidence in courts of law.

9
The End of an Era

Attempts had been made by several groups and agencies, as well as by individuals, to follow the official instructions and live in amity and kindness with the Aborigines. All had failed. To some, the solution was simple—the Aborigines were a dying race: they *had* to give way to white man's civilization. All the white man could do was to care for the natives in their last days. One settler expressed the view:

242 . . . that nothing can stay the dying away of the Aboriginal race, which Providence has only allowed to hold the land until replaced by a finer race. But, while they do remain with us, I consider we are bound to make them as comfortable as we can. They are invariably well treated here. I would recommend the issuing of a few hundred pairs of blankets to them every winter.[1]

At least this writer was a little more compassionate than the members of the Legislative Council quoted at the end of the last chapter.

Others, while still claiming the inevitable extermination of the Aborigines, thought that there was hope with the children—an argument that we saw when considering the very early days of settlement. One settler thought that if the young could be salvaged from the ruin, the race might be preserved.

243 The only method that could be adopted for the instruction and improvement of the natives is, in my opinion, to take away their children to some establishment where they would be entirely removed from the influence of their parents and tribe. Little can be done for the old, except with regard to their comfort. The removal of their children as soon as they are weaned, may appear a harsh proposition, and it would be so to mothers or fathers with keen feelings, but these the blacks do not possess. In most cases, they would be induced to give up their children for a few figs of tobacco, to any one in whom they had confidence, and though they might soon return and wish to recover them, the same bribe would again satisfy them. These educated children would require to be kept

---

[1] C. G. N. Lockhart, in reply to a Circular Letter from the Select Committee on the Aborigines and Protectorate, *N.S.W.L.C.V.P.*, 1849, p. 20.

away till all the old ones had become extinct, which would not be a great many years. This, in my opinion, is the only means of saving the race from extermination.[2]

> Governor Gipps, in looking for a solution to the problem, saw some prospect of success in part of a report made by Captain Grey, who had commanded an expedition into the interior of the north-west of Western Australia.

244 The remainder of Captn. Grey's Report, I am disposed to think by far the most valuable part of it, as it relates to the means by which the Aborigines may be induced to become voluntary laborers for wages.

I consider this the most important part of the Report, because I am myself firmly persuaded that, next to the diffusion of Christian Instruction, the use of money, or to speak more correctly the enjoyments which the use of money commands, are the most effectual of all means that can be resorted to in advancing civilization.

I have on various occasions, and particularly in answer to an address presented to me at Wellington Valley in Novr. last by the Inhabitants of the County of Bligh, endeavoured to persuade the Settlers of New South Wales to look to the Blacks for a supply of Labour.

I have also seriously contemplated the introduction of rewards to persons employing them, somewhat after the manner that is suggested by Captn. Grey, but have hitherto been deterred from attempting it by the fear of the abuses to which such a practice might lead, and the certain difficulties that would attend on the distribution of the rewards.

. . .

It may be right for me however to point out to Your Lordship that my opinions, with respect to the employment of the Aborigines, are at variance with those of many persons, who consider it essential to keep them as far as possible out of contact with White Men.[3]

> Eight years later, La Trobe, Superintendent of Port Phillip, made some observations on the part played by money in 'civilizing' the Aborigines.

245 A sense of the value of money is perhaps the next particular, in which an approach to civilization might be shewn to exist.

Doubtless it does exist—a certain value may be placed on the more sober native in the employ of the settler upon the wages he receives as his reward, and by the frequenters of the town in the

---
[2] Alexander Irvine, *ibid.*, p. 18.
[3] Gipps to Russell, 7 April 1841. *H.R.A.*, I, xxi, p 314.

silver and copper which may be the fruit of his small service, or beggary.

That very considerable sums pass into the hands of certain of the Aborigines, is not to be denied. How these may be dissipated or disposed of, I cannot pretend to say with certainty, but, I think, of this there can be no doubt, that the possession, where it may have been turned to the physical advantage of the holder, has, in no instance, I ever heard of, had that influence over him, which would lead him to throw aside the savage, and seek the advantage of conformity in all important points, to the civilization around him.[4]

> One suggestion made by the Chief Protector during his term of office was that it was essential for the Government to make reserves for the natives before their hunting grounds were entirely taken up by white men. Earl Grey saw several drawbacks to this idea.

246 I am not certain that I rightly understand the meaning of this suggestion for the formation of "suitable reserves" for the benefit of the natives. Among the plans which have been tried in different parts of the World for the protection of Natives in the middle of an advancing population of European Settlers, one has been that of setting apart large tracts of Land as remote as possible from the districts in actual occupation by those Settlers, on which the natives might maintain themselves according to that mode of life to which they were addicted, without interference on the part of the Colonists or of their government. But I think it has been generally agreed that this system is inapplicable to the circumstances of Australia. The necessity under which proprietors of flocks are placed of extending their occupation of Land, such as it is, over wide tracts of Country, in a manner altogether different from the slow process of Agricultural Settlement, the barren and inhospitable character of large tracts of the Australian soil, the migratory habits of the scanty Tribes in search of sustenance which the earth very sparingly affords them, all seem to render the establishment of native reserves of Land on a large scale of very doubtful utility, even if practicable. If, therefore, I am to understand in this manner the meaning of the Chief Protector, it appears to me that, without further enquiry and better evidence than is at present before me, I could not authorize or recommend the adoption of such measures on an extensive scale.

But the very difficulty of thus locating the Aboriginal Tribes absolutely apart from the Settlers renders it the more incumbent on Government to prevent them from being altogether excluded

---

[4] La Trobe to Thomson, 18 November 1848, Appendix to Report from Select Committee on the Aborigines and Protectorate, *N.S.W.L.C.V.P.*, 1849, p. 6.

from the land under pastoral occupation. I think it essential that it should be generally understood that leases granted for this purpose give the grantees only an exclusive right of pasturage for their cattle, and of cultivating such Land as they may require within the large limits thus assigned to them; but that these Leases are not intended to deprive the natives of their former right to hunt over these Districts, or to wander over them in search of subsistence, in the manner to which they have been heretofore accustomed, from the spontaneous produce of the soil, except over land actually cultivated or fenced in for that purpose.

This is a subject on which I wish you to turn your attention. The evil of occasional depredations or acts of violence between Settlers and natives in these outlying districts is one which it is vain to expect can be wholly prevented. But a distinct understanding of the extent of their mutual rights is one step at least towards the maintenance of order and mutual forbearance between the parties. If, therefore, the limitation, which I have mentioned above on the right of exclusive occupation granted by Crown Leases, is not in your opinion fully recognized in the Colony, I think it is advisable that you should enforce it by some public declaration, or, if necessary, by passing a declaratory Enactment.[5]

> The Executive Council had already considered this possibility, and had found it outside their powers to secure free access to Aborigines to lands already leased.

247 Adverting to that part of your Lordship's Despatch No. 24 of the 11th February, 1848, which relates to a provision being made to secure to the Aborigines the free use of unimproved Crown Lands for the purposes of hunting, and in other ways seeking their subsistence as heretofore, notwithstanding the occupancy of those lands under leasehold tenure under the provisions of Her Majesty's Order in Council of 9th March, 1847, I have the honor to report to Your Lordship that, having brought the same under the consideration of my Executive Council, an instruction was, under their advice, given to the Crown Law Officers of this Colony to insert in the forms of Leases for the occupation of lands beyond the settled districts a provision securing to the Aborigines the right adverted to by Your Lordship.

In consequence of this instruction, I received from the Attorney General a letter conveying the opinion of himself and the Solicitor General that no condition securing to the Aborigines the privileges of free access to lands remaining in an unimproved state could

---

[5] Grey to FitzRoy, 12 November 1849, *H.R.A.*, I, xxvi, pp. 225-6.

legally be introduced into the leases of Crown Lands proposed to be granted under the provisions of the Act of Parliament, 9 and 10 Victoria, Cap. 104; but suggesting that Her Majesty might by some future Order in Council authorise the insertion of such a condition in the leases. Having laid this opinion also before my Executive Council, they have recommended that, as a condition to the effect proposed cannot legally be introduced into the leases by the local Government, I should request your Lordship to obtain the requisite authority for its insertion by a further Order of Her Majesty in Council . . .[6].

> Deprived of their hunting grounds, scorning white man's clothes and shelter, the Aborigines were more than usually prone to sickness. When they turned to Europeans for medical help, a need at one time supplied by the missionaries, the response was not always charitable.

248 The Aboriginal Natives have suffered severely during the prevalence of the recent Epidemics in consequence of their having no protection from the vicissitudes of the weather or Medical aid under their sufferings. There have been many deaths amongst them, and some of them the best men of their Tribes. They frequently apply to the Settlers for Medicine, and will take anything that is given them in that way; and there is too much reason to believe that the Dispensing in such cases is both unsuited and injudicious. It has come to my knowledge that sheep medicines have been administered to them, producing violent salivation [which] followed by their inordinate drinking of cold water has caused Death.[7]

> Yet a few philanthropists and thinking men, a few men in positions of responsibility, still went on searching for an answer to the problem after sixty years of failure. They also sought the reasons for failure. One such was La Trobe who in 1848 wrote:

249 It remains for me to give an opinion, under what modification existing arrangements, for the protection of the Aborigines, should be persevered in.

There can be no difference of opinion, between Her Majesty's Home Government, and that of the Colony, as to the imperative duty of watching with the most jealous solicitude, over the interests of the Aboriginal Natives within its territory—or as to the objects, whether immediate or more remote, to which its exertions in their behalf should extend.

---

[6] FitzRoy to Grey, 11 October 1848, *ibid.*, pp. 632–3.
[7] Henry Bingham, Report on the State of the Aboriginal Natives in the Murrumbidgee District, 1 January 1848, *ibid.*, p. 402.

It appears to me, however, one main error, if I may be allowed to use the term, in all the schemes devised at a distance for the protection and reclamation of the Aborigines, is to be remarked—namely, that of taking for granted, what a real acquaintance with the Colony, and the form assumed by its Aboriginal races, shews to be unfounded; and this is, that the Aboriginal Natives will submit, in a greater or less degree to your guidance. That when the particular object aimed at is manifestly for their physical comfort, and advantage even, they will consent to follow as and where you lead.

I think that the statement I have given, of their actual position as a race at this date after all outlay incurred, and pains taken, will shew that this is not the case.

Vigorous coercion has never been tried—but neither entreaty nor example, nor cajolery, not even internal conviction drawn from actual experience of the real kind intentions of the Government and better classes of Europeans towards them, and of the advantage of submission to a new system, will strip the savage of his natural appetites and propensities, or make him a willing participant in the advantages held out to him.

I have stated that actual coercive measures have never been tried. Their employment is not consistent with the spirit of the age. But I am sure that if anything would retard the decline of the Aboriginal races of this Colony, and give promise of moral and physical improvement, and development, it would be the employment of such coercion.

The older classes may be past reclamation, and little can be done for them, beyond affording protection and aid, whenever and wherever requisite. But the introduction of a general system of enrolment of all men of certain age,—and of subjection to strict Military discipline, under arrangements which would render their service, wherever employed, as consonant to their peculiar tastes and talents as possible, would, I am convinced, be the only method of introducing a permanent change in their habits of life. and of securing the proper opportunity of inculcating better christian and moral principle. While, with the children, nothing short of an actual and total separation, from their parents, and natural associates, and Education, at a distance from the haunts and beyond the influence of the habits and example of their tribe would hold out a reasonable hope of their ultimate civilization and Christianization.

But, as the adoption of such measures is open, it must be admitted to some real as well as to much ill-founded objection, apart from the obstacles in the way, the question must still be asked, What is to be done?

I think it has been shewn that the expectation that the Aboriginal Natives might under any ordinary circumstances be induced to abandon their natural habits and relinquish their wanderings, is a vain one.

Their right to wander over the pastoral districts in search of food, or of recreation as formerly, never can be justly disputed; and, as the Secretary of State suggests, it appears advisable that especial stipulations, to assure them this privilege, should be made in the forms of leases, to be conveyed to the occupants of Crown Lands for pastoral purposes, under the Orders in Council.

Exclusion from the enclosed and cultivated lands in general, must of course be insisted upon; but the question will not be so easily disposed of, when these are seen to include, as they often will, the river banks and water holes, which have been from time immemorial frequented for pleasure or subsistence by the Natives; and which as long as they perversely adhere to their ancient habits are necessary to their comfort, if not to their existence, in the scantily watered districts of the Colony.[8]

G.A. Robinson, Chief Protector of the Aborigines, placed the blame for the failure to 'civilise' the natives at the door of the Europeans resident in New South Wales: not just the 'lower orders' of Europeans either, but also men 'from whom better things might have been expected'.

250   I do not contemplate, nor can it be reasonably expected, that the Adult Natives will adopt settled modes of existence. They will visit the Stations for short periods, and their stay would be of longer duration were it not for the evil example and influence of the depraved of the white community, and from men from whom better things might be expected; to this cause, chiefly, have missionaries and others attributed the little success resulting to their labors.

The original Inhabitants have strong claims for support: the sick, the aged, the young children are special objects for consideration. The Aborigines are neither mentally nor physically defective, the chief obstacle to their improvement is their gross superstition and prejudices; if these be removed their amelioration must progress. Christian instruction is the only means, and though no conversions have yet taken place, there is no reason to *doubt* but it will succeed.

That the Aborigines are degraded cannot be denied: this is their

---

[8] La Trobe to Thomson, 18 November 1848, Appendix to the Report from the Select Committee on the Aborigines and Protectorate, *N.S.W.L.C.V.P.*, 1849, pp. 8–9.

misfortune, and not their fault; but it is a melancholy fact they have not improved by their connection with Europeans. Loathsome disease of fatal character has spread through all their tribes, vices of the worst description, Debauchery, Drunkenness, and Blasphemy prevail, and is now, since the establishment of Bush Inns, greatly on the increase.

The Aborigines are living with and among these very people, and no permanent good can be hoped for, so long as the depraved of the white population are left without the pale of Christian instruction.

The trifling efforts hitherto made, are as nothing compared with the overwhelming mass of wickedness brought against it.[9]

> This idea had been expressed before on many occasions; no missionary could ever really hope for success when surrounded by convicts. But evidence was placed before the 1845 Select Committee by one witness who compared his missionary experience in Port Phillip—not a penal colony—with that of missionaries to the South Sea Islands.

251 Among no race of savages on the face of the earth are there greater obstacles to contend with; when missionaries have gone forth to other savage nations, they have gone with the words of eternal truth, and a band of pious helpmates; their only obstacles have been the superstitions and vices of the natives; hence truth in the end has prevailed. It is remarked by a valued missionary— "that three white sailors, whom he found on the islands, [had] done more to impede the work of evangelising the natives, than all their superstitious prejudices and vices." If such was the fact, (which I can readily conceive,) what must have been the obstacles and hindrances in the way of converting the natives of Australia, when in the early part of the history of this Colony, nine-tenths were not only unconverted, but felons? Your Committee will duly consider, that the aborigine here has ever been, from his knowledge of white men, blended with those far beneath him in moral debasement, sufficient to thwart the exertions of any missionary, however zealous and devoted. On my arrival at Port Phillip, (not a penal settlement), I found the same hindrance; almost every crack of the whip, and strike of the maul was accompanied with an oath; how differently have been situated the South-Sea Islanders! Hence one failure after another has inevitably followed, which has erroneously created an apathy, even in the minds of the religious world, until prayers for their conversion have comparatively ceased in the congregation of the saints, and the poor Australian savage has been

[9] Robinson to La Trobe, 20 November 1848, *ibid.*, p. 14.

set down as unable to comprehend that there is a God, none thinking or enquiring what obstacles or hindrances are in the way.[10]

The missionaries had found little support from their fellow Europeans. The land-hungry settlers had objected to land being tied up for mission stations, the lower-class whites deliberately undermined the missionary efforts. Colonists had objected to the money spent on the Protectorate System, and to good land being turned into Aboriginal reserves.

A few men of conscience called for sympathetic treatment of the Aborigines, but were told that they were armchair critics who knew nothing about the realities of the situation. The findings of the House of Commons Select Committee handed down in 1837 did not mark a turning point for Aboriginal-white relations in New South Wales. If anything, the situation deteriorated. The various Select Committees held within the colony had as little effect. It is not surprising, then, that the Committee of the Legislative Council appointed in June 1849 to inquire into the condition of the Aborigines in the Colony, concluded their Report with the following paragraph:

252 In conclusion, your Committee wish to express their opinion that, without underrating the philanthropic motives of Her Majesty's Government in attempting the improvement of the Aborigines, much more real good would be effected by similar exertions to promote the interests of religion and education among the white population in the interior of this Colony, the improvement of whose condition would, doubtless, tend to the benefit of the Aborigines.[11]

---

[10] W. Thomas, Reply to a Circular Letter, Select Committee on the Condition of the Aborigines, *N.S.W.L.C.V.P.*, 1845, p. 56.
[11] Report from the Select Committee on the Aborigines and Protectorate, *N.S.W.L.C.V.P.*, 1849, p. 2.

Selected Secondary Sources

For a general background to Aborigines before the coming of the white man students should consult R. M. and C. M. Berndt, *The World of the First Australians*, Sydney, 1964. This book gives an introduction to the traditional life of Aborigines, and has an excellent bibliography. D. J. Mulvaney's article, 'The Australian Aborigines 1606–1929: Opinion and Fieldwork, Part I (1606–1859)', *Historical Studies*, Vol. 8, No. 30, May 1958, is also most useful. (This article is reprinted in *Historical Studies: Selected Articles*. First Series, 1964.)

A few nineteenth century works have been reprinted or presented in facsimile editions in recent years. Some are listed here, with original date of publication in square brackets:

James Bonwick, *The Last of the Tasmanians: or, The Black War of Van Diemen's Land*, [London 1870] Adelaide, 1969;

Peter Cunningham, *Two Years in New South Wales*, [London 1827] ed. David S. MacMillan, Sydney, 1966;

Edward M. Curr, *Reflections of Squatting in Victoria then called The Port Phillip District (From 1841–1851)*, [1883] Melbourne, 1965;

John Morgan, *The Life and Adventures of William Buckley*, [Hobart 1852] ed. with introduction by C. E. Sayers, Melbourne, 1967;

Watkin Tench, *Sydney's First Four Years, being . . . A Narrative of the Expedition to Botany Bay and A Complete Account of the Settlement at Port Jackson*, [London 1789 and 1793] Sydney, 1961.

There are few works specifically on missionaries. Rev. Osmond Thorpe, *First Catholic Mission to the Australian Aborigines*, Sydney, 1950, tells the story of the Passionist Fathers at Stradbroke Island in the 1840s. Ben W. Champion's article, 'Lancelot Edward Threlkeld. His life and work 1788–1859', *Journal and Proceedings of the Royal Australian Historical Society*, Vol. XXV, 1940, as its title suggests, is a biographical article, which includes the story of Threlkeld's mission to the Aborigines at Reid's Mistake. Another article well worth consulting is H. N. Nelson's 'The Missionaries and the Aborigines in the Port Phillip District', *Historical Studies*, Vol. 12, No. 45, October 1965. He questions some of the interpretations made by Mulvaney in the article noted above. N. J. B. Plomley (ed.), *Friendly Mission: The Tasmanian Journals and Papers of George Augustus Robinson 1829–1834*, Hobart, 1966, is a massive work based on Robinson's own writings, telling the story of his work in Van Diemen's Land before he became Chief Protector of Aborigines.

For studies of the Protectorate System, see E. J. B. Foxcroft, 'The New South Wales Aborigines' Protectorate, Port Phillip District, 1838–50', Part 1: *Historical Studies*, Vol. 1, No. 2, October 1940; Part 2: *Historical Studies*, Vol. 1, No. 3, April 1941; and A. S. Kenyon, 'The Aboriginal Protectorate of Port Phillip', *Victorian Historical Magazine*, Vol. 12, 1927–1928.

Recent books on the Aborigines include: Henry Reynolds (ed.), *Aborigines and Settlers*, Melbourne, 1972—a book of documents covering the period 1788–1939. C. D. Rowley's book, *The Destruction of Aboriginal Society*, Canberra, 1970, deals with almost the whole period of Australian history: however, the early sections on the missionaries and the Protectorate are sketchy. Bernard Smith's *European Vision and the South Pacific 1768–1850*, Oxford, 1960, is an interesting examination of the attitudes of white men to native peoples, as expressed through art. *Racism, The Australian Experience*, edited by F. S. Stevens, Vol I, Sydney, 1971, is largely concerned with the study of anti-Chinese, anti-Semitic and anti-migrant views, but there are a few references to the Aborigines. Robert Travers, *The Tasmanians: The Story of a Doomed Race*, Melbourne, 1968, looks at the possible origin of the Tasmanians, and their fatal confrontation with the white man. John Cleverley, *The First Generation; school and society in early Australia*, Sydney, 1971, contains a chapter on the early attempts to educate Aborigines.

Index

Aborigines (individuals)
  Abaroo 21; Black Tom 53;
  Bundle 40; Charley 48, 49;
  Cochran 71; Daddy 48;
  Goongeen 71, 72; McGill 72;
  Musquito 39; Pemulwoy 40;
  Tedbury 40
  (tribes), Bangerangs 61, 62;
  Branch 37; Tautgort 133
Aborigines' Protection Society, 80, 81, 138, 139
Adelaide, 50, 138
Alcohol, 6, 10, 64, 66, 95, 153
Atkins, Judge-Advocate, 128, 129, 130
Australian, 54, 74, 115

Bathurst, Earl, 22, 24, 25, 27, 28, 130
Bigge, Commissioner, J. T., 3, 23, 29
Black Town, 29, 30, 57, 59
Bourke, Governor Sir Richard, 9, 93, 131
Brisbane, Governor Sir Thomas, 3, 60, 86
Broughton, Bishop (formerly Archdeacon), 60, 75, 76, 78, 79, 80, 99, 100
Burton, Mr Justice W. W., 9, 24, 41, 48, 49, 139, 140

Cartwright, Rev. Robert, 17, 27, 28, 29, 57, 58
Charles 11, 1, 2, 3
Coates, Rev. Dandeson, 8, 65, 66
Colonist, 53, 55, 56, 81, 101
Church Missionary Society, 8, 65, 91, 98
Clarence River, 50
Cook, James, 3, 13
Cowper, Rev. William, 59

Crook, William, 14
Cunningham, Peter, 20, 32
Curr, Edward, 17, 19, 61, 63

Dangar, Henry, 46, 47
Darling, Governor Sir Ralph, 3, 6, 7, 29, 42, 69, 90, 130
Dowling, Judge, 137
Dredge, James, 19, 61, 111

Executive Council, 41, 42, 43, 44, 45, 49, 98
Exeter Hall, 144, 145

Fort Wellington, 41, 42

Gazette (*Sydney Gazette*), 25–6, 29, 32, 40, 58, 59, 74, 75, 78, 87
George III, 2, 3,
George's River, 37, 38, 39
Gipps, Governor Sir George, 12, 43, 44, 49, 51, 109, 111, 112, 115, 117, 118, 119, 122, 133, 136, 137, 140, 141, 142, 143, 147
Glenelg, Lord, 44, 49, 51, 65, 109, 111, 130, 132
Grey Earl, 148, 149
Grey, Governor (S.A.), 51, 66, 67
Gunther, Rev. James, 17, 68, 69, 91, 93, 95, 96, 97, 98, 99, 104
Gunther, Mrs, 68, 69, 95
Gwydir River, 44

Handt, Rev. J. S. C., 21, 68, 70, 72, 91, 92, 93, 104
Handt, Mrs, 92
Harper, John, 18, 59, 87
Hawkesbury River, 35, 36, 39, 129
Hill, Rev. Richard, 27, 29, 93

House of Commons, 8, 9, 17
  Select Committee 1837, 1, 4, 9, 10, 11, 43, 60, 106, 107, 109, 131, 132, 133, 154
Humanitarian Movement, x, 1, 106
Hunter, Governor, 37, 127, 128
Hunter River, 52, 54
Hurst, Rev. Benjamin, 66, 67, 133, 134, 138

Johnson, Rev. Richard, 21, 83

King, Governor Philip Gidley, 4, 5, 15, 38, 128

Lake Macquarie, 88, 89, 90, 104
Lang, Rev. Dr J. D., 17, 18, 80, 83, 84, 106, 107, 122
La Trobe, Charles Joseph, 66, 73, 112, 116, 117, 118, 120, 121, 124, 133, 134, 147, 150
Legislative Council, ix, 110, 121, 136, 140, 141, 143, 146
  1838 Committee on Aborigines, 32, 89
  1845 Select Committee, 16, 63, 81, 122, 153
  1849 Select Committee on Aborigines and Protectorate, 62, 123, 126, 154
Leigh, Rev. Samuel, 74, 75
London Missionary Society, 14, 16, 88, 89, 142
Lowe Robert, ix
Lutherans, 100, 101

Macquarie, Governor Lachlan, 22, 23, 24, 25, 27, 57, 74, 79, 81, 88, 90
Maoris, 15, 20, 70
Marsden, Rev. Samuel, 20, 21, 23, 40, 82
Mitchell, Major Sir Thomas, 130, 131, 132, 143
Moreton Bay, 50, 80, 91, 100, 101, 104
Murray River, 50, 51
Myall Creek, 46, 47, 49, 51, 133

Native Institution, 17, 22, 24, 25, 26, 27, 29, 32, 57, 74
Native Police, 120, 121, 122, 124
Noble Savage, 13, 16
Normanby, Marquis of, 138, 139, 140, 141

Parramatta, 22, 24, 25, 27, 29, 32, 37, 38, 39, 40, 49, 57, 69
Paterson, 35, 36
Philip, Governor Arthur, ix, 2, 4, 14, 34
Polding, Bishop, 63, 81, 101
Porter, William, 67, 68, 99
Port Phillip, 44, 45, 46, 50, 51, 62, 80, 99, 103, 104, 109, 111, 116, 117, 118, 121, 122, 124, 133, 135, 147, 153
Prostitution, 64, 65, 66, 67

Reid's Mistake, 72, 88
Robinson, George Augustus (Chief Protector), 109, 111, 112, 114, 116, 117, 119, 125, 126, 148, 152, 153
Roman Catholic Mission, 101, 102, 103
Russell, Lord John, 12, 141

Schmidt, Rev. William, 16, 100
Scott, Archdeacon T. H., 6, 7, 29, 30
Shelley, William, 22, 23, 24,
Shelley, Mrs, 32
Stanley, Lord, 12, 51, 103, 105, 119, 120, 137, 143
Sydney Herald (later *Sydney Morning Herald*) ix, 54, 144, 145

Threlkeld, Rev. Lancelot, 72, 79, 88, 89, 90, 91, 142, 143
Tench, Captain Watkin, 14, 74
Thomson, Edward, 98, 136, 137

Van Diemen's Land, 53, 56, 83, 108, 110, 114, 117

Walker, Rev. William, 19, 20, 31, 32, 59, 86, 87, 109
Watson, Rev. William, 65, 68, 69, 71, 91, 92, 93, 95, 96, 98
Watson, Mrs, 69, 92
Wellington Valley, 59, 65, 67, 68, 70, 71, 91, 92, 95, 96, 99, 100, 103, 104, 118, 147
Wentworth, William Charles, ix, 144, 145
Wesleyan Missionary Society, 18, 20, 26, 86, 87, 99, 100, 103
Willis, Mr Justice, 135, 137

Yate, Rev. W., 16, 69